Australia

MANAGING EDITORS
Amy Bauman
Barbara J. Behm

CONTENT EDITORS
Amanda Barrickman
James I. Clark
Patricia Lantier
Charles P. Milne, Jr.
Katherine C. Noonan
Christine Snyder
Gary Turbak
William M. Vogt
Denise A. Wenger
Harold L. Willis
John Wolf

ASSISTANT EDITORS
Ann Angel
Michelle Dambeck
Barbara Murray
Renee Prink
Andrea J. Schneider

INDEXER
James I. Clark

ART/PRODUCTION
Suzanne Beck, Art Director
Andrew Rupniewski, Production Manager
Eileen Rickey, Typesetter

Library of Congress Number: 88-18337

2 3 4 5 6 7 8 9 0   97 96 95 94 93 92

Library of Congress Cataloging-in-Publication Data

Giacoma, Cristina, 1954-
  [Australia. English]
  Australia / Cristina Giacoma.

  — (World nature encyclopedia)
  Translation of: Australia.
  Includes index.
  Summary: Describes the geographical features, climate
and plants and animals of Australia with emphasis on their
interrelationship.
  1. Ecology—Australia—Juvenile literature. 2. Biotic
communities—Australia—Juvenile. [1. Ecology—Australia.
2. Biotic communities—Australia. 3. Australia.]
I. Title. II. Series: Natura nel mondo. English.
QH197.G4413 1988 574.5'.264'0994—dc19   88-18376
ISBN 0-8172-3325-3

Cover Photo: Gerry Ellis—Ellis Wildlife Collection

WORLD NATURE ENCYCLOPEDIA

Australia

Cristina Giacoma

RAINTREE
STECK-VAUGHN
L I B R A R Y

Austin, Texas

CONTENTS

6 INTRODUCTION

9 AN OVERALL VIEW

The Form and Structure of Australia, 9. The Climate, 11. The Tropical Region, 13. The Cold Temperate Region, 14. The Mediterranean Region, 18. The Semiarid Region, 20. The Arid Region, 23.

25 THE GEOLOGICAL EVOLUTION

The Geologic History of Australia, 25. The Formation of the Ancient Elevations, 26. The Separation of Australia, 29. Relics of the Past, 31.

33 THE GREAT BARRIER REEF

The Reef-Builders, 33. The History of the Barrier Reef, 33. The Life of the Reef, 35. The Colorful World of Tropical Fish, 38. Colonies of Seabirds, 40. Sharks, 42. The Underwater World, 43. The Changing Barrier, 45.

49 THE MARSUPIALS

The Evolution of the Marsupials, 49. The Ecology of the Marsupials, 53. The Kangaroos, 60. The Reproductive Strategies of the Marsupials, 63. Social Organization of Marsupials, 68.

71 THE RAIN FOREST

Hike in the Rain Forest, 71. The Ground Birds, 72. The Professional Suitors, 73. The Australian Everglades, 78.

83 THE EUCALYPTUS FORESTS

The Humid Areas, 83. Birds of the Eucalyptus Forest, 84. Parrots, 85. Other Birds of the Open Forests and Thickets, 91.

93 THE DESERT

Animals of the Arid Zones, 93. The Dingo, 95.

99 THE HUMAN PRESENCE

The Culture of the Aborigines, 99. Changes Brought by Humans, 102

105 GUIDE TO AREAS OF NATURAL INTEREST

Western Australia, 108. Northern Territory, 109. Queensland, 112. New South Wales, 115. Victoria, 118. South Australia, 118. Tasmania, 119.

123 GLOSSARY

126 INDEX

128 PHOTO CREDITS

INTRODUCTION

Hundreds of years before Australia was discovered by European explorers, geographers suspected that land existed in that area. They thought that the known land areas were too unevenly distributed. For that reason, they guessed there must be some areas that had not yet been discovered. They were right, of course, but they had almost no idea what the undiscovered lands looked like. As a result, the oldest map of what is now known as Australia shows a huge continent covering nearly half the world.

Unlike this 1587 map, Australia is actually the smallest continent. It lies in the area where the Indian Ocean meets the Pacific Ocean.

For sixty-five million years, Australia was isolated from other lands. Land animals that lived there carried their young in pouches or laid eggs. Australia once was nearer to a series of island groups. These islands reached all the way to Asia. They served as "stepping stones" for many other kinds of animals. These animals, including humans, moved into Australia. People began living in Australia only twenty-five thousand years ago.

Because Australia was isolated so long, some of the forms of plants and animals that live there are now extinct in other parts of the world. A kind of plant or animal is said to be extinct when it has died out, for whatever the reason.

Often, extinction is related to a process called evolution. Evolution is the way plants and animals are believed to have changed over millions of years. Plants and animals tend to change in ways that help them survive.

In Australia, evolution has produced some very unusual animals. The many kinds of kangaroos are a good example. Some of these hopping animals are only a few inches long, while others are as tall as humans.

The theory of evolution is mostly based on the study of rocks and fossils or traces of early plants and animals. The world's oldest fossils and rocks have been found in Australia.

There are still many clans of native Australians. These people are called aborigines. Many of them continue to live in the old way. They refuse to accept the ways of the white people. Instead, they try to follow customs that began thousands of years ago.

AN OVERALL VIEW

A close look at a map shows Australia as a compact continent. From north to south, it is 2,300 miles (3,700 kilometers) long. It is 2,548 miles (4,100 km) wide from east to west.

Except for its northern coast, Australia is surrounded by a deep ocean. Around the north coast is a wide continental shelf that is not very deep. Along the eastern coast, the area of the Coral Sea, stretches the Great Barrier Reef. This reef consists of islands and huge accumulations of sea plants called corals. It is more than 1,200 miles (2,000 km) long.

Australia is the flattest continent on earth. It consists mostly of plains and plateaus, with occasional hills that have been worn down by erosion. The most impressive mountains are the Australian Alps. In the winter, one area of the Australian Alps is covered with snow. This area is greater than the entire surface of Switzerland, and it has become a favorite place for skiing and other winter sports. Compared with North America, Australia's seasons seem reversed. Winter begins in June. The hottest months are from November to March.

The Form and Structure of Australia

The entire continent can be divided into three basic units. These are the Western Plateau, the Central Lowlands, and the Eastern Mountain Chains.

The Western Plateau has an elevation of between 984 and 2,297 feet (300 to 700 meters). Its central part contains very old riverbeds that are usually dry. Water runs there only during the rare times when it rains. In the south the rainwater gathers in low areas, forming mud that is later covered by a crust of mineral salts. The salts are left behind as the water evaporates. The northern and the southern coasts are the only zones of the Western Plateau that are crossed by streams. These empty into the Indian Ocean.

The lowest part of the Central Lowlands is Lake Eyre, which is 49 feet (15 m) below sea level. This lake collects water from rivers that drain an area measuring 296,000 square miles (768,000 sq. km). In 1939, the lake was described as "an immense white expanse without life nor the probability of renewal." The description and prediction turned out to be wrong. In 1950 and 1974, some unusually heavy rain temporarily filled the lake and attracted many water birds.

North of Lake Eyre are the reddish sandy dunes of the

Preceding page: Shown is a view of Uluru, or Mount Ayers, an ancient rock mass in the heart of the vast Central Australian lowlands. It is 1,115 feet (340 m) in height. Weathering caused by wind, rain, and wide daily temperature changes has created numerous cavities and cracks. Aborigines regard Uluru as a sacred area. They have decorated the walls of many caves with paintings showing rituals and events from their lives. The materials they used were ochre (earthy mineral oxides of iron mingled with clay), ashes, and coal.

Opposite page: A female emu defends her eggs. These are running birds that cannot fly. They live in groups in the dry parts of the Australian interior. Emus are still quite common although they were widely hunted by both the aborigines and later by European colonists. Aborigines hunted these birds for their meat. Colonists hunted them because they destroyed crops.

Rock cliffs touch clouds along the coast of the Indian Ocean in the Great Australian Bight. These 328-foot (100 m) cliffs alternate with large, sandy beaches, thick mangrove swamps, and shallow coves. This varied coastal landscape is inhabited by many kinds of marine and land animals.

Simpson Desert. These are arranged according to the direction of the strongest winds. To the south, there is the Murray-Darling Basin, which is formed by the Murray and the Darling rivers. The Murray is the only river that consistently supplies enough water for such human activities as agriculture. The river has stopped flowing only twice during the last one hundred years. The Darling River is more than 1,200 miles (2,000 km) long. Despite its length, however, it has a very irregular flow. This is typical of Australian rivers. During dry periods, the Darling is reduced to a series of muddy

puddles. But during rainy periods it floods the surrounding areas. After the Darling River flows into the Murray River, the Murray empties into Encounter Bay. There it forms a large marshy area.

The Great Dividing Range, or the Eastern Mountain Chains, is composed of a series of plateaus. These gradually get smaller toward Australia's interior. The side facing the ocean, however, has steep slopes and sheer cliffs. These are the most important mountains of Australia. They extend for about 1,988 miles (3,200 km) from Cape York to the island of Tasmania. The southern part of this range includes the Australian Alps. In the Alps, Mount Kosciusko towers to an elevation of 7,310 feet (2,228 m).

The Great Dividing Range influences the amount of rainfall over the entire continent. The mountains cause the masses of damp air coming from the Pacific Ocean to rise. This creates heavy rainfall in the coastal zone. Once the air masses have moved beyond these plateaus, they become heated and are able to hold more moisture without releasing it as rain.

The Australian Alps also affect the rivers and streams. The streams in the steep coastal areas are fast-flowing. Those on the western side are long and rather slow-flowing. Often the western streams dry up before they can empty into larger rivers or other bodies of water.

The Climate

The Australian climate is arid, which means dry. The arid and semiarid territories cover two-thirds of the entire continent. The lack of rain is partly caused by two things. For one, 40 percent of Australia is in a subtropical zone. This zone has a climate similar to that of the deserts of northern Africa. For another thing, elevations are not generally high enough to cause clouds to release their moisture.

The masses of damp air rarely reach the interior of the continent. When they do, only a small amount of rain falls. An extreme example is the city of Onslow in Western Australia. There, the annual precipitation has ranged between 0.6 inch (15 millimeters) and .04 inch (1.085 mm). Warm dry winds often blow in the interior regions. This causes water to evaporate quickly.

Unlike most of the northern continents, Australia does not have extreme changes with each season. The trees are mostly evergreen, and some species bloom throughout the year. The Australian winter can be surprisingly cool.

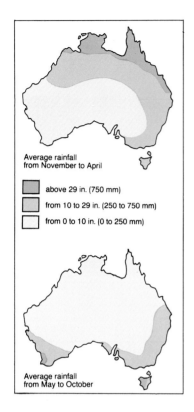

Average rainfall
from November to April

■ above 29 in. (750 mm)

□ from 10 to 29 in. (250 to 750 mm)

□ from 0 to 10 in. (0 to 250 mm)

Average rainfall
from May to October

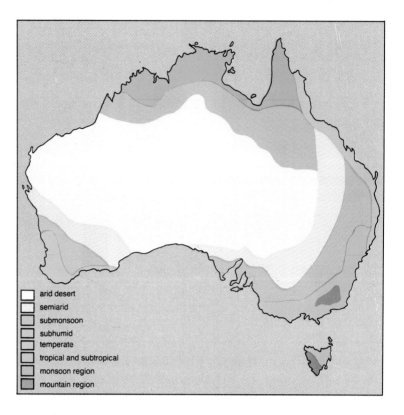

□ arid desert
□ semiarid
□ submonsoon
□ subhumid
□ temperate
□ tropical and subtropical
□ monsoon region
□ mountain region

Above left: Average seasonal precipitation in Australia is illustrated. In spring and summer, which run from November to April, masses of warm and humid air from the northeast cause rains in the northern regions. The air masses gradually lose their moisture while moving toward the interior of the continent. In fall and winter, from May to October, the northern regions are influenced by dry southeasterly winds. On the southern coasts, masses of humid air from the South Pole cause heavy precipitation. The precipitation does not reach the interior.

Above right: Australia can be divided into several climatic zones according to the distribution of rain. These climatic zones partly correspond to distribution of plants. In the tropical, subtropical, and monsoon regions are rain forests and eucalyptus forests. In the subhumid, temperate, and mountain regions are hard-leaved thickets, eucalyptus forests, peat bogs, and mountain meadows. In the submonsoon and semiarid regions are savannahs and thickets of shrubs and dwarf eucalyptus (mallee country). Shrubs and grassy vegetation dominate in the arid region.

The mild climate is affected by the Indian and Pacific oceans. Australia is not large for a continent. Consequently, the affect of the ocean is felt throughout the territory. A branch of the warm Pacific Ocean current along the eastern coast causes the very pleasant climate in that area.

The Australian coasts, especially the eastern coast, are often struck by cyclones. These cyclones are also called hurricanes. They form in the Coral Sea and release their fury as soon as they reach land. Such storms cause serious damage along a 186-mile (300 km) stretch of coast. The *willy willies*, which is a name for the cyclones of the western zone, occur less often.

There are five climatic regions within Australia. These regions are mostly determined by the amount of rain that they receive. They each contain certain plants and animals. Since the rainfall decreases from the coasts toward the interior of the continent, these regions can be shown as circles. They correspond to circular bands of different kinds of plants. The circles are concentric. *Concentric* means that they have a common center and are circles within circles. The circles get smaller near their common center.

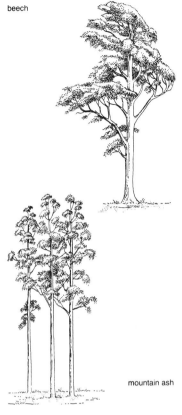

beech

mountain ash

blue eucalyptus

snow eucalyptus

The Tropical Region

In northern Australia, the average monthly temperature does not fall below 59 degrees Fahrenheit (15° Centigrade). Variations by season depend on the amount of rainfall.

In the language of the aborigines, there are words for the sudden changes of season. For example, they use the term *rain weather* for summer. This occurs when warm and moist air arrives from the tropical zone. They call the next season *forbidden weather*. It consists of cyclones and floods that make any kind of human activity difficult.

However, the heat and humidity of this period do cause animals to be more active. There also is an explosive growth of plants at this time.

Native Australians call the season that follows *burned grass weather*. Then the strong rays of the tropical sun rapidly evaporate the water. This dries the plants. The dried-up brush and grass are burned by aborigines hunting wild animals. The fire drives the animals out of hiding. Aborigines call winter *cold weather*. Next comes the *warmed up weather*, which is followed by the new rains as the seasons repeat. Because the weather changes so rapidly, the first explorers that described this region gave reports that seemed to disagree with each other.

The most spectacular plant areas of the Australian's tropical region are the forests. These are forests of eucalyptus trees. The continent has more than five hundred kinds of eucalyptus. They are commonly called gum trees. Some species grow as tall as 130 feet (40 m). The undergrowth of these forests consists of plants that sprout, grow, and die during the rainy season.

The tea tree grows along streams. Its white buds are eagerly eaten by many birds. Less abundant are groups of palm trees reaching 65 feet (20 m) in height. There also are cycads. Cycads are ancient plants that now exist naturally only in Australia and Mexico. They resemble the palm tree.

The true rain forests are limited only to areas that offer conditions like those around the Great Dividing Range. There the rainfall is heavy throughout the year. These forests are evergreen and reach a height of 100 to 165 feet (30 to 50 m). Covering their branches and trunks are epiphytes. Epiphytes are orchids and ferns that grow on other plants. The host plant provides support but not food.

Along the coasts of the tropical region are mangrove swamps. These swamps are the most interesting of the

13

A group of snow eucalyptus trees is shown. These small evergreen trees are common in the colder temperate region. Stands of this species are widespread in the Australian Alps at elevations of between 4,265 and 6,560 feet (1,300 to 2,000 m). Life is hard in this cold, windy region. Sometimes the wind sweeps across the slopes with hurricane force. Plant species that do manage to live here are few and highly specialized.

continent because they contain a rich variety of plants and animals.

The Cold Temperate Region

The coldest climate in Australia is found in the southern part of the Great Dividing Range and in Tasmania. During the winter, wet, westerly winds blow across this region. They cause snowfall in the Australian Alps.

The forests of this zone include plants that first grew in Antarctica. These plants were probably more widespread during the periods when glaciers covered large parts of the earth. The gigantic Antarctic beech trees are found in the Macpherson Mountains. There they form a thick forest that also contains giant ferns and tropical palm trees.

In the southern zones of this region, mountain ash trees cover large areas. They reach heights of more than 328

A clump of river eucalyptus trees marks a waterway in an Australian river basin. These trees grow along rivers and streams. Where they grow, there is a stream—either a permanent one or a stream that flows only after heavy rains. In years of low rainfall, these rivers are reduced to a series of pools. A surprising variety of birds finds refuge among the branches of these majestic eucalypts, which can reach a height of 98 feet (30 m). When the trees flower, the air rings out with the songs of honeyeaters, which flock to the trees in search of nectar.

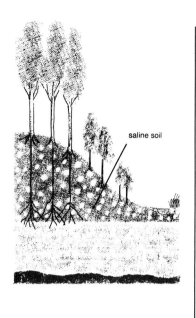

saline soil

feet (100 m). Their trunks are very large in diameter. Along with the sequoias of the west coast of the United States, they rank as the largest trees in the world. The undergrowth is rich with maidenhair ferns and orchids.

The very dense forests gradually give way to more open forests. The open forests vary greatly from one zone to another. In the many valleys and gorges of the Blue Mountains, there are numerous forests of blue eucalyptus trees. In the mountain forests are stands of snow eucalyptus. This eucalyptus is a short and twisted evergreen. It grows best at elevations between 4,300 and 6,500 feet (1,300 to 2,000 m). At these elevations are also the karri trees and giant eucalyptus trees.

Many species of plants live and reproduce successfully in this area. This resulted from evolutionary changes that made them able to stand the cold. Some of these changes resulted in small size and underground trunks. Flowers often form entire "cushions." These also help protect the plant from the cold. When the snow melts, the flower cushions in mountain peat bogs offer a fine show of colors.

The Mediterranean Region

The climate of Southern Australia resembles that of the Mediterranean in Europe. It is fairly mild, and there is frequent precipitation during the winter. The most interesting area of this zone is the wet eucalypt forest. Farther north, this eucalypt gradually changes to what is called a rain forest. The wet eucalypt forest has plants that are very stiff. They hold their shape even after the plants dry up. Some of the common plants found here include myrtles and ilexes. Their leaves are covered by a waxy layer which controls evaporation.

The eucalyptus trees of this region form forests so thick that the leaves of the side branches are always in shade. Because of this, the side branches fall off, leaving a long bare trunk with a plume of leaves at the top. In the western Mediterranean region, there are forests of tuart, jarrah and karri trees, whose white trunks can reach a height of 330 feet (100 m).

Giant ferns grow in the thick undergrowth of shrubs of these forests. The root system of the jarrah tree is well-suited to the spongy soils of the hills where it grows. It has roots near the surface as well as roots that grow deep into the ground. The shallow roots trap rainwater, while the deep roots anchor the tree and reach underground water. These

Opposite page: Shown is an illustration of the damaging effects of the cutting of the jarrah forests. Until fifty years ago, these trees were widespread in the hills of southwestern Australia. The jarrah tree has both surface roots and deep roots that penetrate to underground water *(top).* These deep roots help maintain the water table at a constant level. The uncontrolled cutting of these trees allows more rainwater to seep into the soil. This raises the underground water level. The water then penetrates the soil and dissolves the mineral salts *(middle).* The water, now polluted with mineral salts, seeps through the ground and collects in low areas and rivers. It kills plants and gets into drinking water. Later attempts at replanting jarrah and trees *(bottom),* have not been successful. The growth of the jarrah was slowed by a fungus that developed in the soil.

Right: Pictured is the flower of the ''kangaroo paw,'' a plant that is commonly found in thickets of eucalyptus. Its stems reach a length of 3 feet (1 m).

19

Helichrysum apiculatum

blue devil

trees are cut over large areas for lumber. As a result, underground water rises closer to the surface. The water carries the salt away. This pollutes the streams and rivers.

Another completely different forest of the Mediterranean region is the dry eucalypt forest. There the trees are further apart. More sunlight can get through. There are also more side branches on the trees.

The Semiarid Region

This is a huge zone between the coasts. The region is directly influenced by the oceans, as well as by the internal desert of the continent. This zone has less rainfall as it extends from the coasts to the interior. At the same time, the average annual temperature becomes warmer from the coasts inland. This causes evaporation. Consequently, the plants are distributed in circular bands of plains and bush country. There are very thick stands of mallee, or dwarf eucalyptus bushes. Farther inland are mulga or thorny acacias. These are tropical trees with branched leaves and tight clusters of small yellow or white flowers. In the next band of plants are clumps of spinifex, which are grasses having spiny leaves and seeds.

Opposite page: Arnhem Land is a broad plateau in northern Australia. The landscape changes dramatically with the seasons. In summer, the rains form vast marshes. But at the season's end, the water quickly evaporates. The ground dries out. The marshes disappear. At the few spots that hold any water at all, dense thickets crowd around.

Above: A marsh interrupts the monotonous landscape of the Australian savannah or plain. These moist zones are extremely rare in the arid regions. For this reason, they attract many animals including water birds, Johnstone crocodiles, and freshwater turtles.

In grasslands of the savannah are scattered groups of acacia trees and a certain type of oak found only in Australia. It is a member of the genus Casuarina. The leaves of this oak are small scales wrapped around threadlike twigs. Unlike the related African acacia trees, the Australian acacias do not have thorns. Species of eucalyptus trees that can live in dry climates are also found in this zone.

Regions of grasslands without trees are rare. The variety of plants changes greatly from zone to zone. This change depends partly on the elevation and soil of an area. Kangaroo grass was one of the most important types of plants for the plant-eating animals of the desert. At one time, it was very widespread. Now it survives only in the areas where there is no heavy grazing by domestic cattle or sheep. This grass, which is native to the tropics, only grows in the summer. By then, the other plants are already tall. This allows the kangaroo grass to survive grazing by native animals but not by flocks or herds of livestock.

Mitchell grass is the most abundant grass of the northern plains. In the next band of plants are yellow fields of a type of grass scientists call *Helichrysum apiculatum*.

An expuanse of spinifex is pictured. These grasses are very common in the drier regions. Occasionally, their ball-shaped clumps extend for hundreds of miles. Their leaves are rigid and needlelike. They are used by aborigines to make hunting weapons.

In the driest zones, plains and brush are mixed with dwarf scrub woods of plants that can live in very dry areas. There is almost no underbrush or grass. This tangle of shrubs consists mostly of short treelike mallee and mulga shrubs.

In the language of the aborigines, mallee means "impenetrable." In fact, these eucalyptus shrubs have a swollen, woody stem that is mostly underground. It is called a tuber and looks something like a potato. From this tuber grows a bush of several trunks. This bush forms a rather dense tangle.

The dwarf eucalyptus has ways of surviving the dryness and poor soils. The leaves hang downward, directing the movement of the dew toward the soil. There, a thick layer of fallen leaves acts like a garden mulch. It insulates the soil from the direct rays of the sun, keeping it cool and moist. Roots branch out horizontally from the woody tuber. They are able to absorb the moisture that collects on the ground during cool nights. Other roots grow deep down to the water that exists underground.

Eucalyptus trees manage to grow quickly after fires. Fires often occur in these scrub woods because of the thick layers of very dry fallen leaves. The seeds of many eucalyptus trees survive fires because they are covered by a thick capsule. They grow easily in the areas that have been cleared by fires. After a fire numerous buds in the woody tuber spring to life. These buds produce new shoots. The shoots sprout among an amazing variety of flowers. Within five years, the eucalyptus crowds out the other plants of the undergrowth. After ten years, dwarf eucalyptus trees form a dense 26-foot (8 m) high wall.

The river eucalyptus is another common plant of the semiarid region. It needs more water and is found in muddy riverbeds. It has a sturdy root system that resists the force of the water when the river is full. It is a majestic tree that reaches 82 feet (25 m). The trunk of the river eucalyptus is spotted with gray, white, and red.

The Arid Region

One-third of the Australian continent irregularly receives less than 10 inches (250 mm) of rainfall annually and is subject to wide changes in daily and yearly temperatures. Yet, there are few zones that are completely without life.

These areas include temporary streams or saltwater pools in which grow plants that can tolerate a great deal of salt. The leaves of these plants sparkle. They are shiny from the salts that are passed through the leaves after they have been absorbed by the plant.

Most of the desert grasses use half as much water as required by most plants. Australian plants that grow for more than two years (perennials) have many ways of saving water or using only a little of it.

In years of abundant rainfall, occasional outbursts of flowering plants show up among the perennial plants. They grow only when water is available and they die off within a few weeks.

THE GEOLOGICAL EVOLUTION

Australia appears to be an island of calm surrounded by groups of smaller islands that are continuously experiencing volcanic eruptions and earthquakes. The continent is stable because it rests securely at the center of a hard portion of the earth's crust. This is called a tectonic plate. On the edges of this plate, currents of molten rock form. These come to the earth's surface creating areas of volcanoes, hot springs, and earthquakes.

Australia's fields of cooled lava and volcano cones are extremely old. These lava fields and cones have crumbled into small fragments. This shows that long ago the continent was very unstable. Evidence of this can be seen in the basaltic rocks and the trachyte rocks. These were formed from molten rock. These rocks can be found in various areas of the interior desert. The cones of volcanoes which were active 100,000 years ago can be seen in parts of the Great Dividing Range of mountains.

The Geologic History of Australia

The world's oldest rocks have been discovered in Australia. From them geologists have estimated that the earth is more than four billion years old. Even more surprising is the discovery in some of these rocks of traces of early forms of plants that lived three billion years ago. These organisms resemble the blue-green algae that still live in Shark Bay, a bay that faces western Australia. The bay's concentration of salt was too high for other kinds of marine life to develop.

Very few fossil remains of the first animals without backbones have been discovered. This is because the animals' delicate tissues did not hold together long enough to become fossils. (Fossils often consist of mineral salts which replace the bones of a dead animal or the stem of a plant. This is why fossils of soft-bodied animals are rare.) Several fossils have been found in the heart of the Australian desert and in the Flinders Mountains. These were fossils of animals resembling the present-day sea pens and twenty-five species of jellyfish that lived 600 million years ago.

At that time, the ocean covered small and large areas of north-central and eastern Australia. The water gradually receded to expose the land mass. When the sea fell back, huge deposits of marine life were left behind. Many fossil impressions of early fish, which lived in the sea 400 million years ago, appeared. They are found in several hills of the central desert. This desert is called "Gogo" by the aborigines.

Opposite page: Carved by time, steep walls form narrow gorges across the ancient Australian highlands. They were formed over millions of years by the action of wind and water. The cavities and ruts show where soft layers interlace the hard. The soft areas are the first to wear away.

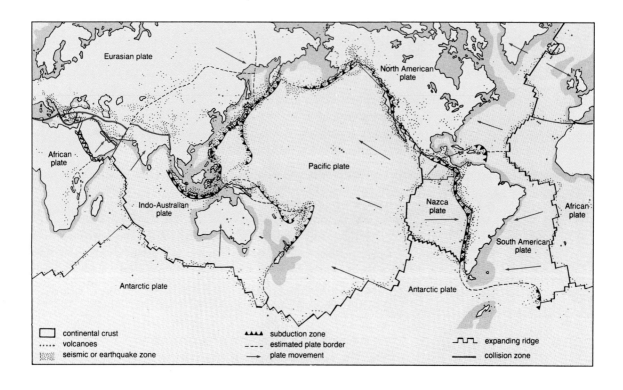

The illustration shows eight of the main plates. Labels visible on the map include: Eurasian plate, North American plate, African plate, Pacific plate, Indo-Australian plate, Nazca plate, South American plate, African plate, Antarctic plate, Antarctic plate.

Legend:

- □ continental crust
- ····· volcanoes
- seismic or earthquake zone
- ▲▲▲▲ subduction zone
- - - - estimated plate border
- → plate movement
- ⅃⊓⅃⊓ expanding ridge
- —— collision zone

How the earth moves: Scientists identify fifteen plates in the earth's crust. The plates are continuously moving. The illustration shows eight of the main plates. Plates generally have three types of edges: *expanding ridges,* where the plates separate from each other and new material fills in; *subduction zones,* where one plate slips below another; and *collision zones,* where continents carried on plates collide. The map shows how the areas of earthquakes and volcanoes are concentrated in narrow, connected bands. These areas are affected by the edges of the plates and their movements. This explains why Australia is so calm; it is isolated from areas having earthquakes and volcanoes. Instead, it rests securely in the middle of the Indo-Australian plate.

The Formation of the Ancient Elevations

The best-known high point in Australia is called "Uluru" by the aborigines. Europeans named it Ayers Rock. It is a 1,100-foot (335 m) high hill of sandstone. According to the aborigines, it was formed at the beginning of life. They call the period the "time of dreams," which to them is the past, present, and future. Geologists date the rock back to the beginning of the Cambrian period, 550 million years ago. It was a period of warm seas and deserts. In that time, layers of rock called "arkose" were deposited horizontally. Arkose is a type of sandstone. Later, movements of the earth's crust tipped these layers nearly on end. They now run nearly vertically. No one knows how these rocks reached the center of the continent. The most probable explanation is that they were formed by the erosion and the sediments carried by one of the numerous ancient seas.

The Kimberleys mountain chain contains rocks that have been changed by intense heat and pressure. These are called metamorphic rocks. The Kimberleys are a chain of rough hills in the north part of the continent. They have only recently been explored. Most of Australia's gold deposits have been found in these rock formations.

The Macdonnell Ranges, in the heart of Australia, are

Erosion is at work in plateaus and rounded peaks of the Great Dividing Range or Eastern Chains. This range parallels Australia's eastern edge. The side facing the ocean consists of steep rock cliffs 656 feet (200 m) above the water. These mountains were eroded by the torrential rivers such as the one shown here.

among the oldest mountains. Their backbone is composed of "metamorphic" rocks that were formed more than 600 million years ago. Various layers of limestone and sandstone were deposited over these rocks. The mountain building process continued until 200 million years ago, near the start of the Triassic period. When the mountains were formed, they reached 16,400 feet (5,000 m) in elevation. In that same period, plants and amphibians moved onto dry land.

In 1971, an expedition of plant scientists traveled to the gorge of the Genoa River. There they found the traces of the oldest known land animals with a backbone. The traces had been left there about 350 million years ago by an amphibian measuring about 3 feet (about 1 m) in length. Previously, fossils of this fishlike creature had been found in Greenland. The wind and rain eventually wore away the outer layer of rocks of the Macdonnell Ranges. For about 100 million years, this process cut slowly into the harder rocks that make the backbone of the ranges. Spectacular gorges were created.

Finke Gorge's natural amphitheater was cut by the ancient course of the Finke River. It is the longest river in Australia's interior. It is 375 miles (600 km) long, and it dries up and disappears at the southwestern edge of the Simpson Desert. In the past, it flowed 995 miles (1,600 km), and it formed deep and narrow canyons in the Macdonnell Mountains. In these gorges, the climate remains cool in contrast with the surrounding desert. Plants that have survived in this relatively cool climate may once have lived throughout the entire region. If they did, the climate of this desert must have been completely different then.

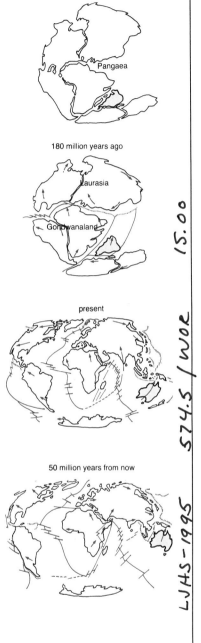

200 million years ago

Pangaea

180 million years ago

Laurasia

Gondwanaland

present

50 million years from now

Adrift on a sea of molten rock, continents have moved. The changing flow of the molten and magnetic forces caused the Pangaea supercontinent to split off into Laurasia and Gondwana. The Australia-Antarctic block later separated from Gondwana. The present arrangement of the earth's continent developed about 65 million years ago. The lands are still moving.

The Great Dividing Range nearly summarizes the geologic evolution of the entire continent. It is composed of a complex combination of various types of rock formations from different geological periods. Over hundreds of thousands of years, these formations have been raised up, folded, and worn away. The granites are among the oldest rocks. They were formed 350 to 400 million years ago. The limestones contain fossils that date back 200 to 300 million years ago (the Silurian and Devonian periods).

Geologists believe that about twenty million years have passed since the first uplifting of these plateaus. They also believe that another uplifting, accompanied by a rotation of the mountain, occurred at a later time.

The steep drop and rapid flow of streams and rivers that empty into the Pacific Ocean in this area seem to support this explanation.

The Separation of Australia

The study of the magnetic fields of rocks formed 300 million years ago in the late Carboniferous period shows that the continent moved. As a result, the climate became considerably colder. This was during a period of forests and amphibians.

Australia was originally part of a gigantic continent called "Gondwanaland." Until 200 million years ago, this continent united all the lands of the present Southern Hemisphere. These were South America, Africa, India, Australia, and Antarctica. About 100 million years ago, a series of deep cracks in the interior of Gondwana resulted in the separation of India, which migrated toward Asia. Later on, South America and Africa separated and began moving west, away from the Antarctic-Australian block. South America was already separated from Africa when the cracks occurred. About sixty million years ago, this allowed Australia to start drifting north. The northward movement of Australia also caused a series of climatic changes.

For a large part of the Mesozoic period, between 70 and 180 million years ago, the heart of the Australian continent was covered by the sea. This sea entered the continent from the north at the Gulf of Carpentaria. All of the dry land was fertile and was covered by jungle and scattered lakes. The lakes were formed by rivers that ran down from the eastern and western hills. These two sets of high areas rose to form two large islands.

Even though the first mammals had already appeared

Below: Palm trees like these were discovered in 1872 within the gorges of the Macdonnell Mountains. The existence of these palms in this isolated area seems strange at first. This species was one of Australia's main plants millions of years ago. About sixty million years ago, there was a vast sea in the central part of Australia. One of the coasts of this sea was composed of the slopes of the Macdonnell Mountains where palms now seem out of place.

Opposite page: Along with the palms and cycads, *Eucaliptus papuana* is one of the primitive kinds of plants that grew in Australia millions of years ago.

in Australia, the dominant animals of the Mesozoic period were the dinosaurs. Fossil remains of the meat-eating *plesiosaurus* have been found in the arid expanses of inner Australia. This 43-foot (13 m) giant apparently was an excellent swimmer. Its head measured almost 10 feet (3 m), and it had an armored mouth with numerous rows of teeth. Giant plant-eating dinosaurs such as the *rhaetosaurus* and the *austrosaurus* roamed the plains. They were more than 32 feet (10 m) long.

The plants and animals of the eastern and western coasts of Australia were separated from each other during a large part of their evolution. The main barrier that separated the plants and animals was the sea. Later other barriers appeared. These included the dry desert of the central part of the continent and variation in soils.

Relics of the Past

After the dinosaurs died out in Australia, there was a continuous evolution of the marsupials. Marsupials are animals that carry and nurse their young in pouches on the mother's body. These pouches shelter the young until they are fully developed. Some well-known marsupial animals are the opossums and the kangaroos.

About one million years ago, during the Pleistocene period, huge ice sheets called glaciers moved across parts of the earth. Climates became colder and colder. The interior lakes and rivers became dry. Animals that were common in tropical forests and rivers either became extinct or survived in very small areas. These smaller areas had conditions similar to those of the Miocene period of thirty million years ago.

The freshwater *Craterocephalus* fish of the ancient past was probably widespread over Australia. Today, it only lives in New Guinea and in several springs of an oasis in Australia's Simpson Desert. This oasis is one of the few permanent pools of water which have remained in the desert interior.

The gorges of the Macdonnell Ranges still have many kinds of animals that were widespread over Australia one million years ago during the Pleistocene period. Today, they manage to survive only in the narrow gorges formed by the erosion of the streams.

Many expeditions have been organized in this area. They were searching for evidence of changes in climate that have occurred over geologic times. These climatic changes led to the near extinction of some plants, as well as the extinction of some kinds of wombats and giant kangaroos.

In these gorges are primitive plants called cycads. They have not changed over the past 200 million years. Palm trees 100 feet (30 m) tall were discovered in 1872 by Ernest Giles along a tributary of the Finke River. They are the only descendants of the trees that grew on the shores of the great interior sea millions of years ago.

These palms have seeds that are too heavy to be carried by the wind. The fact that they exist there indicates that at one time all of that region must have had other plants typical of hot, equatorial climates. Recent discoveries of several primitive fish confirm the past existence in this zone of species that could not have arrived by migrating across the desert. They are called "relics" of a period in which the living conditions were entirely different.

THE GREAT BARRIER REEF

The Great Barrier Reef is a maze of coral banks and islands off Australia's northern coast. It faces open ocean that is 1 mile (1,600 m) deep. This huge structure is 1,200 miles (2,000 km) long and 200 feet (60 m) deep. It is composed partly of the skeletons of animals. Many of these animals are reef-building polyps. Many of these polyps have jellylike bodies that are shaped like cylinders. One end is often attached to a solid surface. The other end is an open mouth that is surrounded by many stinging tentacles. Some polyps take on the resemblance of fragile flowers. They live together in groups called "colonies." Such colonies often have a hard covering that serves as a skeleton. There are other building blocks of reefs. These include the shells of animals called "mollusks" plus deposits left by such soft-bodied animals as jellyfish and worms and by plants called "algae."

The Reef-Builders

There are corals scattered among all the oceans, but nearly all of the true reef-building corals are found in tropical waters. They prefer areas warmed by ocean currents. There the water temperature does not fall below 73°F (23°C). One such place is the northern coast of Queensland. Here, every year the polyps form a new layer of what is actually limestone on top of the existing layers. Under the best conditions, a reef can grow at a rate of 10 inches (24 cm) per year. To do this, the polyps must eat large amounts of microscopic floating plants and animals. These tiny organisms are called "plankton." Clouds of plankton float in the sea of the Great Barrier Reef.

For fast growth, the coral colony requires plenty of oxygen and nitrogen. These compounds are produced by algae. The algae absorb carbon dioxide. The process forms limestone. This, in turn, makes up the outer skeleton of the colony. The importance of the algae in this situation partly explains why corals are found at depths of less than 66 feet (20 m). Below that depth, there is not enough light to allow the algae to function.

Besides the corals, there are other soft-bodies marine animals that are able to form outer skeletons or shells. They do this by hardening calcium.

The History of the Barrier Reef

Today, scientists are still learning how the 1,240-mile (2,000 km) long and 200-foot (60 m) deep Barrier Reef was

Opposite page: Snorkelers tread water over the Great Barrier Reef off Australia's northern coast. The best way to appreciate the beauty, variety, and richness of the barrier is to snorkel or scuba dive.

formed. For one thing, corals normally can not live deeper than 65 feet (20 m). So how can the Barrier Reef be 200 feet (60 m) deep? Again, scientists must look at the area's geologic past. Piles of fossils 1,800 feet (550 m) high have been discovered. One is at Wreck Island in Australia's Capricorn Islands. The building of this bank must have been started by the ancestors of the present-day polyps. This was about one billion years ago. Because the evidence is so old and incomplete, it is hard to tell exactly how the Barrier Reef was formed. More than one hundred years ago, Charles Darwin suggested one way it may have happened.

Charles Darwin was an Englishman who sailed around the world from 1826 to 1850 on a ship named the Beagle. During the trip, he worked on a theory about how plants and animals changed over long periods. Darwin became very interested in coral reefs. At first, he was puzzled. How did plants and animals that could live only in fairly shallow water build reefs that were so deep? He decided that the ocean floor was sinking. Darwin said that the reefs were built as fast as the floor sank. In this way, he said, colonies of coral added to the top of the reef while the bottom slowly dropped.

There is another theory. It is that the sea became shal-

Shown is the outer margin of the Great Barrier Reef. Beyond, toward the open sea, it is a one-mile drop (1,600 m) to the bottom. Here the reef is exposed to all of the destructive force of the ocean waves. As a result, corals with the toughest and more compact skeletons are the most abundant in this part of the reef. The border between the ocean and reef becomes less obvious during high tides. The reef is then under water. As the tide moves in, deep-water fish such as barracudas and small sharks come to feed.

lower during the Pleistocene epoch. Supposedly, moving ice called "glaciers" cut away the bases of coasts and the coral reefs. The present coral reef would have been formed in layers as the ocean became deeper.

Darwin's theory is more convincing. Recent evidence has been found proving that the ocean floor has sunk. Geologists agree, however, that the shape of the reef was affected by the last glaciers, twenty thousand years ago. Today, there still are unanswered questions about exactly how all of the living and nonliving forces that build and maintain the Great Barrier Reef fit together.

The Life of the Reef

Some pointed fragments are broken from the coral reef by the action of tides, waves, and wind. The ocean currents cause these bits of coral to accumulate. These form small, flat islets called "cays." There are more than seventy of these cays along the Barrier Reef. Each one is very different.

The small plane carrying visitors to a cay of the Capricorn Islands nears the ring of rocks encircling the beach. The plane lands on a strip of coral fragments. The coral has been cemented together. Even during low tides, the reef is never completely dry. There are puddles of water up to 7

feet (2 m) deep. These puddles contain whitish outer skeletons from the coral colonies. Some of the rock areas seem velvety. But an up-close look will show thousands of small fluttering tentacles that capture microscopic animals.

During the day, the cay's surface can be seen clearly. There are fans, giant leaf shapes, mushrooms, and small funnels. At night, the polyps extend from their hard coverings, revealing their colors and intricate shapes. The cay is alive with color. There are deep fire reds, deep blues, pinks and violets. In the sheltered areas are branched corals and colorful soft corals.

In many pools are starfish of a deep blue color. Despite their beauty, they are efficient killers. With their arms they can open the shells of large shellfish that are embedded in the rocks. Inside the half-opened shellfish are the brilliantly colored bodies. They range from purple to emerald green. Some of the shellfish are very big. In the cays and reefs at the north end of the Barrier, some shellfish, or mollusks, have shells measuring more than 3 feet (1 m) across.

Despite the many kinds of animals, life in this part of the reef is hard. It has been called a torture chamber. It has many drastic changes in temperature, salt concentration, and other water conditions. Many organisms are able to take advantage of these changing conditions. Sand stars are one example. These starfish have long, feathery arms that normally capture animals found near the bottoms of the pools. But when the high tide arrives, they raise their arms to capture the food on the surface.

Every type of marine life seems to live in these small pools. There are many sea cucumbers. These look something like rotting cucumbers from a grocery store. Some are reddish purple. Others are brown with a layer of sand cemented to their bodies. Sea cucumbers sift through the sand that accumulates at the bottoms of the pools. Pools contain other animals called sea urchins. Black sea urchins twist their stalks while walking on what looks like pin points. Colorful bodies and glowing eyes appear from within the shells of some animals. Sea worms come out of their tubes and fan their tentacles in search of food.

This wonderland also hides predators such as the cone shellfish. They have compact, smooth shells with delicate colors and designs. From the narrow crack between the two halves of their shells they shoot small darts containing poison. This poison is so deadly that it instantly kills large fish and other animals. It can make a human very sick.

Opposite page: At low tide, the reef reveals its world. As the ocean retreats, the Great Barrier Reef holds back pools of salt water. Many of these pools are more than 3 feet (1 m) deep. They contain a showcase of marine life that is either trapped or looking for shelter. Among them are the colorful starfish, sea cucumbers, giant clams, and many multicolored fish.

Fish of the Great Barrier Reef find safety in numbers. They swim among the corals in large schools. There are more eyes to look for enemies. When an enemy does come, it is discouraged by the confusing mass of fish darting away in every direction. This buys the fish time for escape. Group living is one way in which young fish are protected. When they are old enough to find a mate, they may move off and live by themselves.

Another danger to humans is the stonefish. This is a crusty fish with an irregular shape. It remains perfectly motionless until it is touched by an unlucky animal. It then sticks out its thirteen poisonous needles.

The Colorful World of Tropical Fish

Very colorful barrier fish dart above, below, and across the colonies of reef building corals. A violet trunk fish with yellow dots stops to curiously observe a human diver's hand. A small orange fish exhibits all of its menacing tactics in order to scare away a fish that is intruding in its territory.

The density of fish in these waters is very high. Over two tons (2,000 kg) of fish have been netted in a one-acre area of the reef. Under such crowded conditions, animals must spend a great deal of time finding and defending living space.

Most fish in these waters have brilliant designs and colors that signal their presence. They can be easily recognized by the other fish of their own kind. This can be important to fish that look alike, for many kinds of angelfish have the same shape and size. They tend to live in different parts of the barrier. Even so, each kind has its own showy colors. This seems to help one fish find possible mates. When the time for depositing eggs is near, the eggs of the female must be fertilized by a male of its own species.

When the males are excited, their bodies show certain colors. These colors show up when the males fight. When one of the two rivals gives up, its color pattern changes. This signals the winner that the fight is over. The winner maintains its color through the mating process. At that time, coloring encourages the female to deposit its eggs.

The mating pair often shares the task of defending territory. This is especially true when the eggs are deposited. In other instances, the territory belongs to a group. For example, the male pygmy angelfish defends its territory with the assistance of a whole harem of females. The harem usually numbers about ten females. Sometimes there is even an auxiliary male. When the leading male leaves the group, one of the mature females actually turns into a male! The transformed fish then assumes leadership of the group.

Different kinds of angelfish have different ways of living among themselves. These may depend on the population balance between enemies and the fish competing for food and living space. One kind of angelfish, for example, can change the way it lives. Even though it usually defends a territory alone, it may go looking for help. If certain fish drive it away, it joins a group of other fish of its kind. Sometimes, fish may even join groups composed of several species in order to overcome an enemy. Some predators use the same tactics. To invade areas where eggs are defended by a mated pair, a predator may find help to drive off the defenders.

The lagoons of the smaller coral islands contain many fish that do not compete with the coral eaters or algae. One such fish is the archerfish. It captures flying insects by shooting them down with its own saliva. A relative, *Balistes*

Angelfish are noted for their elegant shapes and beautiful colors. They are among the first fish to catch the eye around coral reefs. Angelfish hide among the corals or swim rapidly in search of algae or tiny animals to eat.

fuscus, is able to feed on the sea urchins of a group called *Diadema.* The urchins have very hard spines. They have a soft spot where they attach themselves to coral. The fish knocks away part of the coral supporting the sea urchin. The fish fires a strong jet of water onto the sea urchin, turning it over. The fish breaks open the urchin's underbelly. This underbelly is the only part of the sea urchin that is not covered with spines.

From October to the end of February, sea turtles land on the sandy island beaches. They come at night during high tide to deposit their eggs. The female scoops out a hole and lays about one hundred eggs. She covers the egg hole with sand and heads for the water. When the eggs hatch, the baby turtles crawl to the water and swim away.

Colonies of Seabirds

Toward evening, the terns return to the coral islands. They occasionally skim the surface of the water as they fly. Their loud calls seem out of keeping with their tapered, slim bodies. There are species of terns that nest on these islands in weedy and bushy areas.

A green turtle cruises the depths of the coral banks. This species lives in Australia's coastal waters as well as in distant parts of the ocean. It normally prefers the surface waters and feeds on plants. Females dig deep holes in the beach about 165 feet (50 m) from the water. They lay their eggs and cover them up with sand. The young hatch after about two months and immediately make their way to the water. Instinctively they know the direction to go. Many never make it. They are eaten by mammals, birds, and reptiles. These losses, along with the more significant harvest of adults for meat by humans, have helped push the species near extinction.

Noddy terns nest in the brush thickets. They build flat nests that are made of leaves cemented together with bird droppings. Noddy terns fish during the day in places that are farther away than the fishing grounds of other terns. When noddy terns fish, they follow schools of tuna. They dive at the schools, causing the fish to flee in every direction. At dusk, the terns fly rapidly between the trees. After several noisy minutes, they settle down for the night on branches.

From October to April, many muttonbirds or shearwaters return from the sea. Once they find their colony, they begin to descend while calling out to their companions. They land on the ground, because their nests are in burrows. The entrance of the nest has a diameter of 4 inches (10 cm) and reaches a depth of around 3 feet (1 m). A chamber is formed in which the egg is laid.

As more birds arrive at the colony, there is a tremendous increase in the chirping, shrieking, and wailing. These are noises which only bird lovers would be able to appreciate. The nightly calm returns to the island in April, when the mated pairs of shearwaters abandon the plump chicks. The chicks are not yet able to fly. However they are fat and manage to survive until they are able to leave the nest.

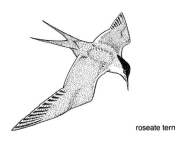

roseate tern

sooty tern

noddy

silver gull

Seabirds are very important in the spread of plants among the small coral islands. Their droppings, which are called "guano," fertilize the ground. The seeds of many plants are also contained in the guano. They quickly sprout and grow in the fertilized soil.

Birds like the noddy tern feed on the fruits of heliotrope trees. They do not digest the seeds. They pass the seeds back out of their bodies. In this way the seeds, which otherwise would decompose rapidly, are carried from one island to another. As a result, the heliotrope tree is widespread.

Sometimes, too many plants grow. This limits the space available for the birds that nest on and under the ground. These birds include the gulls, the terns, and the shearwaters. These birds face another serious threat from rats. Rats came in as stowaways on ships. They have spread rapidly. The rats feed on the chicks of the ground-nesters.

Sharks

Many signs of sea life wash up along the beaches. Among the shells and the algae left on the shore by the high tide are fragile "by-the-wind sailors," a type of jellyfish. These have a triangular veil of many glowing colors. The veil helps the jellyfish move. It is attached to a dark blue disk hung with threadlike colonies of tiny polyps. There also are many jellyfish called "pneumatocysts." They are full of gas. These jellyfish trail threadlike colonies of polyps that can be 165 feet (50 m) long. These threads contain poisons that are dangerous to humans.

At high tide, water fills the deepest channels and pools, covering the coral colonies that are closest to the surface. This enables some fish that usually live out in the open waters to come within 165 feet (about 50 m) of the shore. Among these open-water fish are the manta rays and the great reef sharks. The reef sharks have flat bodies. These sharks are not "killing machines." To the local people, reef sharks seem almost friendly. It is possible to tell when this big red shark becomes alarmed. It arches its back and makes threatening movements.

Sharks often carry passengers. One is the remora fish. They have sucking disks that attach to sharks, whales, sea turtles, and ships. The remoras are used by aborigines for capturing sea turtles. A remora is tied to a line and left to swim in the open sea. When it sees a sea turtle, it attaches itself. It does so with its razor sharp teeth. The aborigines are able to capture the sea turtle by hauling it in.

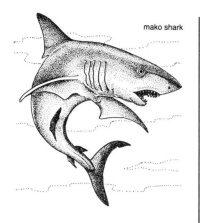
mako shark

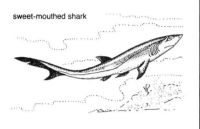
sweet-mouthed shark

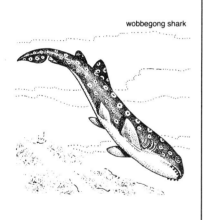
wobbegong shark

hammerhead shark

Recent scientific studies have inspired new ideas about how dangerous and unpredictable sharks can be. Some researchers say that sharks are dangerous and unpredictable only to those who know little about their behavior. One of the myths that has been disproved concerns how "primitive" sharks are and how underdeveloped their brains are. Actually, the shark's brain in relation to its body size is comparable to that of many birds and mammals.

Sharks have proven to be as capable as rats in solving problems and telling different objects apart. Studies of groups of elephant sharks in the Gulf of Mexico have shown that these animals are able to use new hunting techniques. They pass this new knowledge on to other sharks in their group. These sharks, which normally feed only on plankton, have been taught to capture large fish by "standing" with their tail fins downward and keeping their mouths open.

Sharks can swim and feed in water that is very cloudy. When they are unable to see very far, they use sounds and weak electrical fields to identify their food. They also are very sensitive to magnetic fields. This sensitivity works like a compass to help them tell direction.

People who study sharks have found other surprising things as well. One is that the adult female may break away from the group. She is followed by a male. The male bites her on the back. The wound looks more serious than it really is. The bite heals within two weeks. The pair swims side by side and the male fertilizes the female. Then the two return to the group. The females can wait a long time to lay their eggs. This way the female can find the ideal spot to deposit the fertilized eggs.

Humans are a shark's worst enemy. Humans fight them with every means available. One way is with the anti-shark nets that have been set up in the waters off Queensland. These are intended to protect swimmers from attacks by sharks. In a sixteen-year period, these nets killed 20,500 sharks, 2,654 sea turtles, and 468 dugongs (seacows). These last two species are in danger of extinction. Some people believe that the nets are useless. Most swimmers stay out of the water in the tropical summer anyway because the waters are invaded by large numbers of poisonous jellyfish. In winter, most of the sharks move to deeper water.

The Underwater World

Many people dive among the corals to get a close look at the life that abounds there. Some wear face masks and

Two large mantas glide through the waters of the Great Barrier Reef. These batlike creatures normally live in open water. They occasionally enter the waters of the coral reef areas, taking advantage of high tides.

carry tanks of air. This is called "scuba" diving. The letters stand for "self-contained underwater breathing apparatus." With air tanks a diver can descend along the edge of the reef. This wall is almost straight up and down in some places. It has many holes and caves of various sizes. The creatures that are most active at night hide in these places during the day. These include sharks and moray eels.

Animals that should be avoided are more than fifty kinds of sea snakes. They swim through the water, pushing with their flattened tails. Occasionally, the snakes swim near the surface, where the water is warmer. Their poison is deadly, twenty times more powerful than the poison of a cobra snake. It acts on the nerve centers of its victim.

A diver slowly swimming along the reef wall may come close to being run over by a school of tuna fish or young barracuda. Older barracuda are loners. These adults remain motionless, waiting for unwary fish to move far enough from hiding to be captured.

A manta ray may swim slowly past. Its large winglike fins may be 23 feet (7 m) wide. It ripples through the water when it moves along. Despite its size, the manta does not alarm nearby fish. Actually, it feeds on tiny plants and animals called "plankton." Remora fish swim above and below its immense body. The remoras feed mostly on parasites that are attached to the skin gills and mouth of the host fish. While the manta is being "cleaned" of parasites, it provides a safe place for the remora fish. This must be an old relationship because the cleaning fish has special adaptations that help it live with the manta shark or other host fish. Remoras have suckers close to the abdomen or belly that enable them to attach themselves to the host fish.

There are more than forty kinds of fish in these tropical waters that live on the parasites that infest other fish. Many of these cleaning fish are territorial, creating "cleaning stations." Cleaners are permitted to approach their hosts, and may even enter their mouths and gills undisturbed. What messages have the cleaners sent that tell the host to leave them alone? The color of their bodies and the "dances" that they perform aid the host in recognizing its helpers. Recent studies also show that the host fish's sense of touch is especially important. There often is a lot of body contact before the cleaning fish begins its work. These contacts occur only in clear water. This may mean that it is necessary for the two partners to see each other before the cleaning process begins.

There are other cleaning fish similar to the remora in color, striping, and movements. Thus, both types of cleaning fish are allowed to clean two kinds of hosts. This doubles their feeding opportunities.

But the false cleaning fish also is a "false friend." It snatches several strips of the host fish's flesh. The false cleaner also uses this fakery to distract the attention of the host fish from its eggs, which are deposited in holes in the coral. The false cleaning fish also eats its host's eggs.

The Changing Barrier

The Great Barrier Reef is always changing. Plants and animals absorb, filter, eat, and break apart reef fragments.

Sea life on the Great Barrier Reef is pictured. On the surface are two jellyfish (the larger one is a poisonous Portuguese man-of-war). These animals drift with the ocean currents. Below them, a cleaner fish cleans the mouth of a squirrel fish. Nearby, a false cleaner fish, whose striping and colors perfectly imitate those of the true cleaner fish, lies in wait for the unsuspecting host. In the distance, a barracuda hunts. On the bottom, a stonefish and clam ignore the show.

One enemy is the crown-of-thorns starfish. It is one of the most voracious predators. It has seventeen long, spiny arms. This starfish turns its stomach inside out over a coral colony. The starfish uses its digestive fluids to turn the tissues of the coral polyps into liquid. In a year's time, one starfish can digest 65 sq. feet (6 sq. m) of coral reef. This is significant because there are a lot of giant starfish all eating at once. In one area of the Great Barrier, people killed 27,000 of these giant starfish in an attempt to control the damage to the reef. One reason that many starfish come to one area is that they are attracted by the digestive fluids of other starfish.

Sea storms and cyclones, which are common in this tropical zone, can also have disastrous effects on the coral colonies. Staghorn corals are usually the most abundant corals. They often form the only colonies present in an area of reef until a natural disaster such as a hurricane occurs. In only a few hours, several types of algae and other organisms move in. Other new arrivals include the larvae of sponges, other corals, starfish, sea urchins, and sea cucumbers. They all compete with each other for space.

A school of colorful fish hovers in the crystal waters of the Great Barrier Reef. More than 1,500 species of fish live among the sheltering colonies of corals. The chief builders of the reef are uncounted billions of polyps. These soft-bodied creatures attach themselves to a hard surface, then form a skeleton. When the animal dies, its skeleton remains as part of the reef. The polyps can only function in shallow water. Then how can the reef be so deep? One answer is that the ocean bottom sank while the reef formed at the surface.

The fight for survival is very rough. Of the two hundred colonies that are first established in an area of 11 sq. feet (1 sq. m) of damaged reef, only three or four colonies remain after a few years. Some coral colonies send out threadlike "tentacles" that digest neighboring colonies.

One of the biggest causes of change in the Barrier Reef is people. For many years, millions of tourists have come to carry off the reef's natural treasures. Undersea mining and drilling have also taken a toll. Rivers emptying into the ocean have brought silt and chemicals from farms far inland. In 1979, a significant step was taken toward preserving the reef. A portion of the reef's southern end was declared the Great Barrier Reef Marine Park. In the years since then, the park has been protected from destructive human activities and there are now efforts to set aside other portions of the reef.

THE MARSUPIALS

Australia is well known for its unusual animals. Many of these animals are mammals. A mammal is an animal that nurses its young in the same way a cow feeds its calf milk from its udder. Cats, dogs, and humans are mammals. In the entire world, there are only two mammals that hatch their young from eggs in the same way as chickens. These live in Australia. They are the platypus and spiny anteater. In the 1700s, sailing ships returned to Europe with some platypus skins, bones, and eggs. At first, no one believed that such animals could live. They thought that the samples were fake.

It is still not known exactly how these animals reached Australia, nor how their unusual characteristics developed. It is certain, though, that the fact that Australia is an island had a lot to do with the evolution of these animals. Evolution is a theory about how plants and animals changed over many years. The numbers of years are so great that they are measured in geologic time. Geologic time consists of periods that are millions of years long.

The plants and animals present on the Australian island remained isolated from populations on other continents. Much later, Australia drifted closer to the islands of New Guinea. These islands formed a "bridge" between Asia and Australia. New forms of animals, including humans, migrated across this bridge to Australia. The movement of a continent like Australia occurs because of magnetic forces and the melted rock deep inside the earth.

The Evolution of the Marsupials

Throughout geologic history, animals living in areas isolated by oceans, deserts, or mountains developed particular physical forms and acted in certain ways. This happened because the animals could not migrate to other areas or mix with other animal communities. They either adapted to their environment or became extinct.

During a period of fifty million years, many new species appeared on this huge island. As time passed, the differences between the animal populations of Australia and those of the other continents became very pronounced. These differences were so great that Australian animals could no longer have mated with related animals living on other continents. Some primitive species that would have died out elsewhere were able to survive in Australia. It offered a separated environment with relatively few large meat-eaters or competing animals of similar kinds.

Opposite page: A female koala hugs a eucalyptus while her cub hangs on. Koala mothers nurse their young for more than a year. Having fewer young and giving them more care is one of the reproductive strategies found in nature. This ensures survival. Besides, the fact that koala females form strong bonds with their offspring seems in keeping with their toylike appearance. Because they look like living teddy bears, these marsupials are very popular with tourists. Only certain kinds—and ages—of eucalyptus leaves are eaten. When Europeans cleared some of Australia's forests, the koala population began to decline. For years, the animal was hunted for its fur. Now, Australia's millions of koalas have been reduced to thousands. Efforts are being made, however, to preserve this animal and increase its numbers.

Sometimes two very similar species evolve in different parts of the world, yet they are not at all related to each other. Europeans coming to Australia named many animals after those they knew. A good example is the wolf. The gray wolf of Europe and North America *(top)* and a marsupial wolf *(bottom)* are unrelated. It is easy to understand how a person can be misled by using only the common name of an animal. As the illustrations show, the nose of the marsupial wolf is larger than that of the placental wolf. The marsupial wolf has rounded ears. The marsupial wolf can open its jaws wider. The marsupial wolf's rear resembles that of a kangaroo. This is evident by the shorter upper part of the foot and the tail, which is wide at the base.

While Australia remained separate from the other land masses, it drifted north. This caused the climate to change. This separation and change of climate are considered by some to have been principal causes of the extinction of many dinosaurs. Their disappearance, which took place 130 million years ago, allowed birds and mammals to adapt and spread rapidly. The oldest fossil mammal remains that have been discovered thus far belonged to a 4-inch (10 cm) long animal covered with hair. It had a set of teeth that were adapted for eating insects. This animal lived about 200 million years ago.

Early in the evolution of the mammals, only two "lines" survived. They remain today. One is represented by animals that give birth to their young and have true milk glands to nurse them. The other is made up of mammals which hatch their offspring from eggs and have only modified sweat glands to provide liquid food. Both lines can be further broken down into three distinct groups. Like the two evolutionary lines, these groups are based on the ways in which the animals have young and feed them. The groups are monotremes, marsupials, and placentals.

Monotremes are the most primitive because they lay eggs as did their reptilian ancestors. The only living exam-

ples are the duckbill, or platypus, and the spiny anteater. Both live only in Australia. Monotremes had already evolved by the time the first marsupials arrived by way of the island groups.

Marsupials are considered more advanced because they bear partially-developed young and nurse them in pouches located on the mother's body. The first animals of this type to reach Australia were small creatures that were most active at night (nocturnal). They ate insects and eggs.

When the marsupials arrived, Australia had few animals. Several animal species that had lived there had become extinct. The marsupials were able to evolve and spread. Today, there are several types of marsupials. They are insect-eaters, plant-eaters, plant-and-animal-eaters, and meat-eaters.

Placental animals originally appeared in the Northern Hemisphere. They have an important evolutionary advantage. This is the ability to nourish the embryo (an organism in the early stages of development before birth) until it is developed inside the mother's body. This is possible because of the placenta, an organ within the uterus. Nutrients in the blood of the mother are passed through the placenta to the embryo.

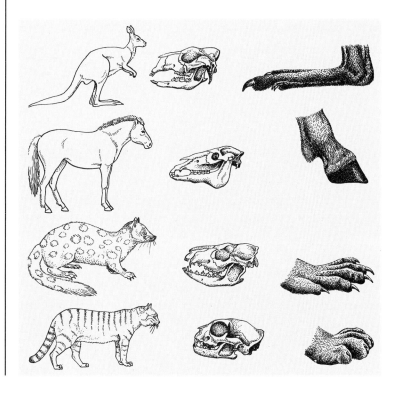

Many marsupials and placental animals have developed certain features related to the way they live. For example, meat-eaters and plant-eaters have specialized teeth and feet. The illustration shows that both the kangaroo and the horse have only one pair of sharp front teeth or incisors. Their feet tend to be small, with fewer toes. These indicate that both animals eat plants and are able to run fast in case of danger. The Asian tiger and the marsupial tiger-cat both have a more complete set of teeth, with several sharp incisors. Their paws have very distinct toes with sharp claws (the claws are retracted in the illustration of the placental cat). Both of these features indicate that these animals are meat-eaters who kill other animals.

Australian native cat

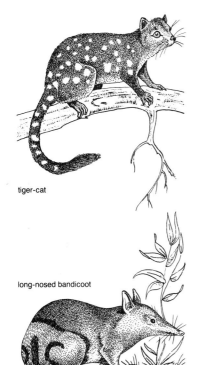

tiger-cat

long-nosed bandicoot

flat-headed
marsupial mouse

Animals with placentas began their own process of spreading and adaptation. They started to move into a larger number of "ecological niches," or portions of the environment. Placental animals are not considered more advanced than marsupials—just different. For millions of years, the two types of animals evolved separately from each other in different parts of the world. But they had to do the same kinds of things in order to survive. This is why some animals in Australia look and act like animals in other parts of the world. This is true despite the fact that they are not related to each other. This is called "parallel evolution."

When the first Europeans settled in Australia, they named the newly-discovered marsupials, or pouched animals, after some more familiar animals that they resembled. For instance, there are marsupials that are called cats, moles, and wolves even though they are not related.

Many marsupials look and act so much like some animals from elsewhere in the world that it is very hard to tell which is which. The marsupial flying squirrel is an example. It looks just like the American flying squirrel. But its American double does not have a pouch in which to carry its young. The marsupial version feeds on leaves. It glides from one eucalyptus tree to to another. Gliding is accomplished by a thin flap of skin. This flap reaches from the front feet to the hind feet. When the animal spreads these flaps, it looks like a square-shaped hawk.

Even more surprising are the marsupial moles. They could easily pass for American moles, which are not related. Marsupial moles have cone-shaped heads. Their eyes are protected by an eye shield. They dig up and eat worms and insects. They seem to "swim" through the ground without leaving a tunnel behind them. Like their American placental look-alikes, they do not have outer ears. Both animals have weak, undeveloped eyes and shiny, golden-red fur. The only major difference between them is the marsupial mole's pouch. This pouch opens downward (instead of upward, as in the kangaroos), thus protecting the young in the pouch from the dirt that is raised as the mother digs in search of food.

Not all the marsupials, however, resemble animals in other parts of the world. One such animal is the koala, perhaps the most popular marsupial in the world. It resembles a stuffed toy teddy bear. Some people call it the "marsupial bear." Others compare it to monkeys and apes because it climbs trees. It also is compared to the sloth

because it moves so slowly. Actually, the koala is entirely different in the way it lives as well as the way it looks. This animal has adapted only to Australia's forests of eucalyptus trees.

Another marsupial that does not look or act like any placental animal is the honey glider, an opossum. It has been called the "hummingbird of the marsupials" because it is among the smallest animals of its class. It glides through the air. Nectar and honey are important parts of its diet.

The Ecology of the Marsupials

When the earlier forms of marsupials reached Australia, they were similar to many species of present day small meat-eaters. They later changed, spread and moved in with the monotremes (egg-laying mammals). Very few fossil remains of the egg-layers have been found. They can best be studied through research on certain present day marsupials.

Later, the marsupial population was greatly reduced by the appearance of the wild dog called the "dingo." Dingoes arrived in Australia about eight thousand years ago. The

The ring-tailed possum is one of the marsupial animals that has best adapted to humans. They are widespread not only in forests, but in Australian cities. The vastness of its territory, which extends along all of the southern and eastern coasts of the continent, has permitted the development of several subspecies. These subspecies are differentiated by the color of their hair.

dingo is a placental meat-eater. It competed for food with such larger meat-eating Australian animals as the marsupial wolf. This competition was surely one of the causes of the extinction of the Australian populations of the marsupial wolf and the Tasmanian devil. In turn, the recent introduction of the fox has had a similar effect on Australia's animals.

The Australian marsupial cats are the species that best hold out against this competition. These include a number of species of tree-climbing predators that have evolved

complicated hunting techniques. One of these animals is the tiger cat, which actually resembles neither tiger nor cat. At most, it resembles a North American marten. Martens are small animals that often are trapped for their fur.

The Tasmanian devil has completely disappeared from the areas where there are many dingoes and foxes. Now it is found only on some islands that belong to Australia. Its name shows that it has never been a popular animal. Its body is square, and its head is large. When it is approached, it growls. But vicious as it seems, it can get along with other animals. In fact, it can be easily tamed. In wild areas, the Tasmanian devil plays a role similar to that of the hyena. It cleans its territory of the bodies of dead animals. It also hunts frogs, snakes, mammals, and an occasional small lamb. Years ago, sheep herders considered this fierce-looking marsupial a mortal enemy.

The bandicoots are ratlike marsupials. They eat insects, seeds, and plants. These animals have teeth similar to those of meat-eaters, but bandicoots do not have as many toes. In fact, most plant-eaters have few toes. This enables the animal to run or climb faster.

Some plant-eating marsupials live in trees. Others live in open spaces. A group called "phalangers" is most abundant in trees. These animals are specialists at living in trees. They have adaptations that enable them to grab tree branches and twigs with ease. The bones of their toes are highly developed. Many phalangers have tails that are adapted to grabbing. Their feet have five toes on large claws. They also have thumbs that can bend and help grasp things. One of the five toes is larger than the other.

Animals that eat plants have specialized digestive systems. Many of the world's plant-eating placental animals have an internal part called a "rumen." Their survival depends on it. A rumen is part of the stomach. It stores food that is eaten quickly. This undigested food is later passed to the mouth to be chewed again. The rumen allows the animal to spend as little time as possible feeding in the open where it is more vulnerable to predators. After feeding, the animal can move to a safer place to chew its food. A rumen also helps to digest plant fibers.

Phalangers and other marsupials do not have a rumen. In Australia, a species can survive without one. This is true because the island is isolated and has few native predators, animals that kill and eat other animals. Even without a rumen, phalangers are able to digest plant and tree fibers.

The illustration shows ways that kangaroos move: 1) while grazing, the kangaroo habitually remains bent over, slowly moving on all four legs and putting most of its weight on the hind legs and the tail; 2) while searching for new pastures or drinking water, the kangaroo moves rather slowly by leaps of about 7 feet (2 m); 3) when frightened, the kangaroo gets into high gear by using its extended tail for balance and making leaps of up to 30 feet (9 m). It reaches a maximum speed of 37 miles (60 km) per hour.

Digestion is accomplished by many helpful organisms called "bacteria." Bacteria live in a phalanger's large intestine. This intestine is unusually long. In the koala, which is a phalanger marsupial, the large intestine can be more than 7 feet (2 m) long.

The better-known plant-eating marsupials are the opossums (Australian species are called "possums" by scientists, to separate them from opossums in other parts of the world). These are small animals with large eyes. They are nocturnal (most active at night). Although they have been widely hunted for their soft, thick fur, the opossums are still fairly abundant. They are widespread because of their remarkable ability to change the way they live. In recent years, they have even moved into cities. At dusk they come out of their daytime hiding places and walk across the roofs of buildings, descending to balconies in search of food.

Marsupials are generally thought to be an unsuccessful experiment of nature. Because of their method of reproduction, they have fewer advantages than the placental animals. As a result, they are widespread only on islands and isolated continents. There is a great deal of evidence that

Speed and endurance are important for animals like these kangaroos. They live mostly in open areas where they can easily be seen by enemies. Although kangaroos can run at a high speed, they are not able to maintain these speeds for long. Jumping with two legs takes more energy than moving on all four legs. If a red kangaroo is chased by a dingo, it cannot keep up the pace. But they are not easily killed. They can defend themselves with their claws and powerful feet.

supports this theory. The North American marsupials virtually disappeared when the placental animals developed in South America and moved northward. For example, meat-eating marsupials bccame extinct in North America three million years ago. This happened when the placental meat-eaters migrated north across Panama. This is very similar to what happened in Australia. There, the larger meat-eating marsupials did not survive after the arrival of the dingo. The inability of some marsupials to compete with other mammals is not the fault of the way they reproduce. More likely, this failure was caused by competing for food and living space.

The placental animals that dominated the Northern Hemisphere actually went through two periods of mass extinction. This allowed more specialized groups of animals to replace primitive species. However, this did not occur in South America and Australia. There the marsupials continued to exist in their early forms until the placental animals arrived. Therefore, the marsupials were not specialized enough through evolution to compete with the northern animals. As a result, the northern animals prevailed.

Changes in living conditions can affect the success of a

Red kangaroos lead a quiet family life. A young kangaroo peeks out from the pouch, or marsupium, of its mother. The young animal is too big to get in and out of the pouch very easily. The male is much larger than the female red kangaroo. Males reach 6 feet (2 m) in height and 176 pounds (80 kilograms) in weight. When danger threatens, the heavier males are the first to be overtaken by predators. As a result, the females, which are important for the continuation of the species, are more apt to get away.

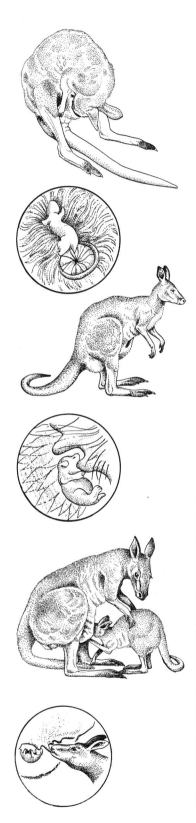

species. This is shown by the relatively recent spread of the Virginia opossum of North America. This opossum has a remarkable ability to adapt to areas that have been changed by human activities, such as agriculture and the building of cities. It successfully competes with mammals and is now very common. Although the meat-eating marsupials became extinct in South America three million years ago, there are nevertheless about sixty-five species of opossums that exist today alongside the other kinds of animals in that continent. Furthermore, the Bennett kangaroo of Australia adapted well in England. Attempts have been made there to start a wild population.

The Kangaroos

The spread of the kangaroo family dates back thirty million years to the Miocene epoch, when Australia's climate was warmer and dryer. The forest that covered the continent began to thin out, and it was eventually replaced by the savannah, a grassy plain with shrubs and small trees. This was a more open area where the animals were vulnerable to predators. The herbivores that succeeded in living in the savannahs had to be able to spot predators quickly. They had to quickly flee and hide themselves in the open areas.

The kangaroos developed a special solution to these problems. Through evolution they acquired an erect posture and powerful, jumping legs. By then, the kangaroo rat, which is widespread in Australia, had already developed these features. It is possible that this was tied to the need to see across a wide range of territory. From such a vantage point, a possible predator could be easily spotted. The young also could be more securely held upright in the mother's pouch. These abilities are such an advantage that it is hard to understand why the kangaroos are the only plant-eaters that have developed powerful hind legs.

The kangaroo's long and powerful tail is also very useful. It is used for balance when the animal is fleeing. The tail of the large species grows more than 3 feet (91 cm) long. When the embryo is only twelve days old, the young kangaroo uses its front legs to climb up the body of the mother to reach the pouch. At this time, the front legs are more developed than the rear jumping legs. Soon, however, the hind legs become much stronger than the front.

Kangaroos are able to jump well because of these highly-developed hind legs. Normal traveling (jumping)

Right: A female red kangaroo nurses her young, although it is really too big to be nursing. This shows the strong bond between the mother and her offspring. The mother and her young often hug and groom each other.

Opposite page: The principal phases of the development of a young kangaroo are illustrated. *At the top:* About one month after mating, the female prepares for birth by carefully licking a trail to the inside of her pouch, or marsupium. She lies on her back to help the hairless, blind embryo as it climbs upward toward the pouch *(top detailed drawing).* Once the embryo reaches the pouch, it is nourished by the mother's milk. After about six months, the youngster looks more like a kangaroo, complete with hair. It then is ready for its first contact with the outside world. But once it leaves the pouch, it often returns to nurse. As it nurses and grows, it may share the pouch with a new embryo that has just been born *(bottom drawing).*

61

One reproductive strategy consists of investing all of the animal's energy in producing the greatest number of offspring. The young are later abandoned. This strategy is characteristic of species that are highly adaptable and, thus, are more widespread. The small marsupial broad-footed mouse uses this strategy. The young become mature in June. The males often fight with each other to claim territory and mates. Mating occurs in September. The males die shortly afterward from sickness and loss of energy. The females give birth at the end of October. The young are nursed until February. Then the male offspring are driven away. The female young are permitted to remain within the mother's territory.

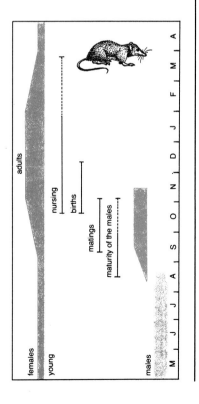

speed of groups of kangaroos is 9 to 12 miles (15 to 20 km) per hour. In the event of danger, the kangaroo can reach speeds of 37 miles (60 km) per hour. But unlike such hoofed animals as the African gazelle, it cannot maintain this speed for very long. At this high speed, jumping takes more energy than running. Kangaroos walk by using the tail and all four legs. This is actually more tiring than when the animals move using the two hind legs or all four legs. This explains why jumping is the kangaroo's preferred way of traveling.

In open spaces, kangaroos usually eat as fast as they can. They swallow their food without even chewing it. The food is stored in the part of the digestive system called the "esophagus." Kangaroos then go to a safer, more comfortable place. There they bring the food back into their mouths so they can chew it. The storage place inside the kangaroo works very much like the rumen, or special stomach of placental plant-eaters such as deer and cattle. This is an example of how evolution has helped animals do the same thing in different ways. It is called "convergent evolution."

Because a kangaroo must chew a lot of grass, its teeth get worn quickly. But this is not a problem. A kangaroo's teeth can be replaced up to four times.

In Australia there are kangaroos that have adapted to many kinds of living conditions. For example, some species of small rock wallabies live in the cracks of the Flinders Mountain Range. These graceful animals have dark hair and ringed tails. Humans almost destroyed the entire population for the animals' fur. Individual species are hard to identify, because these wallabies sleep during the day. They remain on guard in front of their shelters, which they enter at the slightest hint of danger. With luck, one may see them grazing at dusk, before they nimbly jump away among the rocks. They are well adapted for their way of life. The granular pads on the soles of their feet and their short claws help them grip the rocks securely. These short claws provide a small but stable base that is similar to the hoof of a horse or deer.

Some species called "hill kangaroos" have settled in the plateaus, or high level areas. They are able to eat tough grass during any season, while some other animals can only eat it just after it has sprouted.

Tree kangaroos are species adapted to living in trees. They have thick fur, which protects them from the frequent rains in the tropical forests. Their front legs are longer. This helps them move among tree branches. Their claws are

A small jumping marsupial mouse. This species is present in the plains and margins of the desert in western and southern Australia. It is now very rare, and its survival is endangered by the spread of wild cats and rats. Its hind legs are longer than its forelegs, but it rarely moves by using only the two hind legs. It prefers to move on all fours.

Following page: The canine phalanger is a small marsupial that is found mostly in the rain forests of the Great Dividing Range. It is most active at night, and it spends a large part of the day hidden in tree cavities. It comes out only after dusk in search of the plants on which it feeds.

strong and well developed. But even with these advantages, the tree kangaroos are not able to climb trees as well as the phalangers. Tree kangaroos evolved in an area in which there were few competitors and enemies. Therefore, they did not have to develop the same features as the phalangers. If competitors and enemies had been present where they lived, the early tree kangaroos might possibly have evolved into a different form and way of life.

The Reproductive Strategies of the Marsupials

Present-day marsupials continue to have young and care for them in the same way their ancestors did. This consists of giving birth to an embryo that has barely begun to develop. Soon before the birth, the mother carefully cleans the inside of the pouch and lies on her back. The newborn climbs from the mother's body to the pouch, where it is nourished by the mother's milk.

Kangaroos have a remarkable ability to control the development of their young. The offspring generally are reared one at a time. However, the female can care for three

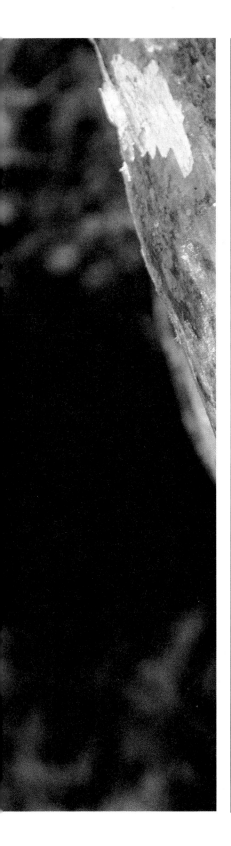

young kangaroos at different stages of development at one time. One might be an embryo inside the mother's body. Another could be newly born and nursing in the pouch. Another could be older but not yet willing to abandon the protection of its mother.

The kangaroos are not considered inferior placental mammals. They have merely developed a different kind of reproductive system. Placentals invest a relatively large amount of time and energy in pregnancy. For example, some of the world's deer have a pregnancy (gestation period) that lasts six or seven months. In contrast, kangaroos are pregnant only twenty-seven to forty days. A newborn kangaroo is much less developed than a newborn placental animal. Consequently, it is not able to care for itself as well. Evolution has provided a way for kangaroos to compensate for this. Kangaroos, with their marsupial pouches, have become specialized in nursing and protecting their offspring while the young continue to develop.

The female gives birth to an embryo that weighs only .03 ounce (1 gram). For this reason, the next stages of development of the young take longer among marsupials. This system also permits the pregnancy to be interrupted at any stage of the development. This may occur during a drought or other condition not favorable to the birth or growth of the young.

Placentals, on the other hand, have some advantages during pregnancy. For one thing, the embryo is more highly developed and more likely to live. This increases a species' potential population. Such an increase in population allows the placental animals to settle in a new area faster than the marsupials.

For example, after a big fire in the Nadgee Reserve in New South Wales, few animals remained. The field mice, which are placental mammals, were the first to colonize the burned area. They were followed by rats. Later the rats almost completely replaced the field mice. It was not until five years after the fire that one of the two species of marsupial mice that originally inhabited the reserve was able to reestablish itself there.

Basically, evolution has provided animals with one of two strategies for having young. In one, an animal invests most of its energy in producing the most young. These babies are soon abandoned. This is the most critical period in the growth of young marsupials.

The other strategy provides for the development of

Two Matschie tree kangaroos are pictured. The tree kangaroos are not particularly well adapted to life in the trees. They move rather slowly and awkwardly among the branches. Fortunately for them, these kangaroos do not have to look far for food in the lush rain forest. Another reason these awkward animals survive is the fact that they have few natural enemies.

only a few embryos at one time. However, the adults later spend a great amount of energy caring for these young during the first phase of their lives.

Virtually all of the animal species that are highly adaptable and spread easily use the first strategy—to produce the most offspring. An extreme example is the broad-footed marsupial mouse. These mice reproduce only once a year. In February, the females interrupt the nursing of the young and are ready to mate again. One month after mating, they give birth to more young than they can feed. For this reason, the last to be born die of starvation.

During the mating season, the males undergo great changes. Their glands secrete high amounts of chemicals which make them gain weight. During this period the males continuously fight among themselves. This causes a great deal of stress. The stress probably causes the males to be less able to resist disease. Before the birth of the young, many males die from ulcers or various infections.

Both the males and females of the different species of

Bennett tree kangaroo

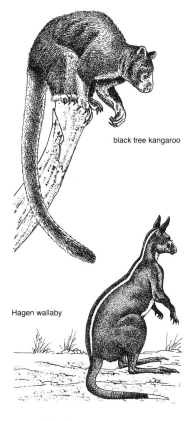
black tree kangaroo

Hagen wallaby

prettyface wallaby

broad-footed marsupial mice devote all of their energy to having the most young during a single reproductive season. The fact that they do not reproduce more times during one season may seem at first to be an obstacle to having the most young possible. Probably the high mortality among males actually is beneficial. It may help prevent animals of one species from mating with those of another. This is called "reproductive isolation." It occurs because, by the time the females of the species that reproduces first are ready to mate, the males of the other species are already dead. Broad-footed marsupial mice are small in size, and have an ability at an early age to reproduce. They live short lives, and the young have a high death rate. These characteristics are generally typical of "maximum number of young" strategy.

With many other animals the females have fewer young. They do not reproduce every year. As a result, they are able to give more time and attention to their young. The koala represents this group of animals. Its young are nursed for more than one year. When the young animal leaves the mother's pouch, the pouch opens downward. The mother then discharges a liquid. It is composed of partly digested eucalyptus leaves.

Some of the koala's characteristics are common to the "fewer young, more parental care," reproductive strategy. These are larger body size, a longer average life span, and mating at a later age. Others are the birth of only one offspring at a time and very selective feeding habits.

The canine phalangers, which can only be found in the rain forest of northeastern Australia, also are included in this group. This animal feeds on plants that live in forest undergrowth. The females nurse their young for nine months and then protect them for another year. The females are not ready to mate again until two years after the birth of their offspring.

There are examples of species that have not adopted the same reproductive strategy as the koala, although they live in the same eucalyptus forests. The fox or vulpine phalangers are found in these same forests, as well as in all the other forests of Australia and Tasmania. These species have adopted the strategy of reproduction which requires the maximum number of offspring. Each fall after their first year of life, almost all of the females give birth. The baby is weaned after six months. Then it is abandoned by its parents. During this period, many of the young die, most of them

males. The females considerably outnumber the males. However, they still mate because the males are polygamous (mate with more than one female). The adults generally feed on a single species of tree.

The flexibility of the vulpine phalangers' eating habits, their high rate of reproduction, and short nursing period enable these animals to rapidly spread into new areas. They can also rapidly settle in areas that have been partly destroyed by fires or human activities.

Social Organization of Marsupials

Only in recent years have scientists been able to obtain accurate information on how marsupials live with each other. This comes from the work of scientists who study animal behavior. A thorough study of this kind is possible only if the scientist is able to identify each member of the group. This is done by learning to recognize an individual or through identification by marking with a dye. The researcher must be able to follow a certain animal throughout the day.

It takes a long time to analyze an animal's behavior. It is necessary to follow a group for a period equal to the length of the average life span for an individual animal of the species. To measure how successful a single individual is at having young, it is necessary to get information during different seasons. Sometimes an animal might behave in ways that normally would reduce its chances of survival. Despite all the research that has been done, scientists are

Male kangaroos quickly establish which one will mate with a female. The illustration shows a fight in progress. At the left before fighting, the two attempt to get each other to back down. This is done by showing a determined, rigid body stance, and scratching and cleaning. If at this point neither male becomes afraid and retreats, the two lock arms. If all else fails, the fight becomes a kicking match.

still a long way from knowing everything about the ways marsupials live.

Some marsupials live in groups; others prefer to live by themselves. Those that tend to live alone defend part or all of their favorite areas. They may even keep out members of their own kind. One example is the male canine phalanger. It defends a territory that partially overlaps with the territory of its mate. "Flying possums" are loners that mark giant eucalyptus trees within their territories with scent signals. Even the animals that live alone generally belong to some sort of central group. This group is formed by the mother and the offspring. The family shares the same area until the young are ready to leave. Then there are fights. Males of the species of broad-footed mice tend to run off as soon as they can survive without their mothers. The young females stay with their mothers.

Shown is the end of a fight between two male gray kangaroos. The two species of gray kangaroos in Australia have different social organizations. The Eastern grays are loners, except for females with offspring. Single individuals have territories that vary in size, depending on the season and availability of food. In contrast, female western gray kangaroos form groups of twenty-five to sixty-five animals. Each group moves within its own territory. The males move within larger territories that overlap with territories of the females. However, the males stay away from the females, except during the mating season.

THE RAIN FOREST

Thirty million years ago, the rain forest probably extended over almost all of Australia. Now it exists only in several parts of the northern and eastern coasts. Plants that long ago came from India and Malaya are the main vegetation of these forests. About ten thousand years ago, certain kinds of trees spread into Australia from Asia by way of the bridge of islands that are now known as Indonesia.

In central Australia, the Asian types of plants are mixed with the Antarctic types. This happened because Australia and Antarctica were once joined.

To reach the rain forest by car, it is necessary to leave the national highway across the eastern coastal region. Steep winding roads lead into the forest. On both sides are trees 165 to 200 feet (50 to 60 m) high. After a few miles, the pavement becomes damp from the layer of fog that condenses on it.

Hike in the Rain Forest

At first, to a hiker, the rain forest seems tiring and disappointing. Clay sticks to shoes. Hikers must climb over the trunks and roots of fallen trees. Some of those obstacles may be as tall as a person. Next come tangles of spiny leaves. In the dark, it is hard to identify all the noises that seem to arise. The trees all look alike. However, when a naturalist explored the area in 1878, he noticed that within the rain forest two trees of the same species seldom grow next to each other. The reason has only recently been discovered. Roots of a plant may release chemicals that slow the growth of other young plants of the same kind. The process is called "allelopathy." It allows a great many different kinds of plants to grow side by side in one area.

Because the rain forest has so many plants of so many different kinds, each plant must compete with others for light. Over millions of years, several species have evolved their own solutions. For example, liana vines climb along tree trunks to reach the sunlight in higher layers of the forest. Many plants rely on other plants for support. These are called "epiphytic" plants. Some of them can survive during dry periods. They absorb carbon dioxide during the night when the loss of water through their leaves is lowest. During the day, the carbon is used to make a type of sugar that the plants need. This process is called "photosynthesis."

Another way of competing was adopted by the "strangling fig." It sprouts on the branches of another plant and gradually kills it.

Opposite page: A dense forest blankets the Tasmanian highlands. Rain forests exist mostly on Australia's eastern coast, from Cape York to Tasmania. Tasmania is separated from Australia by the Bass Strait. Long ago, the two land masses were connected to each other. Their separation has led to the evolution of species that live only in Tasmania. Others once lived in Australia but are now extinct.

Above: The rain forest is so thick that plants grow in layers from the ground to the treetops. Within each layer, or zone, a variety of animals finds refuge.

Opposite page: Like the ostrich and the emu, the cassowary is a running bird. It has its own ways of moving about in the thick undergrowth of the rain forest. For one thing, it is big. It can weigh up to 187 pounds (85 kg). It has strong feet. It also has a type of horny helmet. Like a football player, it lowers its head and charges through the brush *(center)*. The cassowary is shy and prefers to run when alarmed. However, it can stand and fight fiercely if its young are threatened *(bottom)*. Then, it attacks its enemy with the sharp claws it has on the insides of both feet *(detailed drawing)*.

The towering trees of the rain forest provide shelter to many animals. Among them are the tree marsupials, which come out only at night in search of food. The tree kangaroos probably came to Australia from New Guinea. Two of the many tree kangaroos that originally came from Asia have become widespread in Australia.

The rain forest also is home for the cuscus. This is a marsupial with a stout body protected by a woolly coat of hair. Its long tail is very useful for gripping branches while the animal climbs.

The Ground Birds

The ground of the rain forest is a busy, rustling place. Many small wrens and running birds live there. They briskly rummage for food beneath the tall trees.

One of the most interesting forest ground birds is the common cassowary. These birds can only be found in New Guinea and Cape York, the northernmost part of Australia. Cassowaries probably were brought in from New Guinea by the first people to settle there. Cassowary birds are closely

tied to their forest home. They have stout bodies and strong feet. This helps them move about through the underbrush. It is almost impossible to see them because they are silent and cautious animals. Occasionally they can be seen crossing a trail or in clearings that are near streams. They are rather timid, and they flee quickly when alarmed. Their heads are protected by a type of horny helmet, and they have rather poorly developed wings.

The feathers of the common cassowary are long and hard, but they look silky. Like most animals, they would rather run than fight when threatened. But if they are cornered, they will hit their enemy with their prickly wing feathers. The kicks of this bird are also quite dangerous because the inner toe of their foot has a large pointed claw that can cause serious wounds.

A group of birds found only in Australia are the mound-builders. They are called "megapodes." There are three species of megapodes in Australia, two of which, the Freycinet megapode and the brush turkey, are found in the tropical forest.

Mound-builders use one of the simplest nesting methods. The female does not hatch the eggs with its own body heat. Instead, the bird lays its eggs in the cracks between rocks which are well exposed to sunlight. Since the eggs are abandoned soon after being laid, the direct rays of the sun do the work of an incubator. At night, the rocks radiate the heat that absorbed during the day. In this way, the temperature around the eggs remains fairly constant, day and night.

In the forest undergrowth, megapode nests are mounds that can reach up to 10 feet in diameter and 5 feet in height (3 m x 1.5 m). These are made of topsoil and pieces of rotting vegetation. The heat of the rotting plants produces the heat necessary for hatching eggs. Usually, the mounds are reused and enlarged in the successive spring seasons.

The brush turkey uses the same kind of mound for a nest, but it continuously tries to control the temperature of the nest. The male brush turkey often measures the temperature of the nest by poking its open beak into the pile. If the nest is too warm, the bird digs away some of the material to cool it off.

The Professional Suitors

Some Australian birds have amazing ways of attracting mates. Birds of paradise perform one of the most unusual courtships in the rain forest. These birds live mostly in trees.

Four tree kangaroos rest among the branches. Tree kangaroos live in the rain forest. They have thick fur which sheds the rains. Their strong claws enable them to grasp branches. However, tree kangaroos have a tail that is of little use in climbing.

Several kinds eat fruit, insects, and even small mammals. Some birds of paradise are famous for the beautiful feathers of the males. In other species, there is little difference between the males and the females. In these instances, the male mates with only one female and helps build the nest and raise the chicks.

Males of the better-known species have extraordinary colors and elegant forms. They dedicate a great deal of energy to courtship and mating. They do not assist the females in raising and defending the young.

In this area, the males display their colorful, silky feathers by raising and lowering them. They open their beaks and make a whispering sound. They rapidly circle around a branch. Eventually they stop and lower their heads. This goes on for several months. As soon as a female appears, the male mates with her. Mating is over after a few seconds and the female returns to her nest to lay her eggs.

In some species, the most extraordinary features of the plumage are the threadlike tail feathers. The males show themselves off in groups, shaking their feathers. After the

A brush turkey appears in an opening in the woods. It lives mostly in the forests along the eastern coast. The bird builds a mound for a nest. The mound looks like an untidy pile of sticks and rubble. However, it acts as a very efficient incubator. The nest is about 35 to 40 inches (90-100 cm) high and 10 feet (3 m) in diameter.

Pictured is a male satin bowerbird. This metallic-blue bird is common in Australia and New Guinea. It is noted for its "bower"—a structure built to attract females. The male satin bowerbird's bower consists of two walls made of interwoven twigs. The bird decorates it with various objects. It also "paints" parts of the bower with the juices of plants or charcoal mixed with saliva. A piece of bark held in the male's beak serves as a brush.

long mating season, the cumbersome feathers of the male are replaced by lighter-weight feathers that are less showy.

Bowerbirds are found only in Australia and New Guinea. All species have more than one mate, but their method of courting is more practical than the method used by the birds of paradise. The males spend a lot of time decorating their mating arenas. These are stick-walled "bowers" on the ground. There the males patiently wait for the arrival of females. When the females arrive, the males display themselves. If the female enters the arena, they will mate. This behavior probably developed because the bowers helped hide the birds from enemies. Bowerbirds also avoid the hassle of changing to showy feathers each year. This may explain why the males use decorations in their bowers, instead of showy feathers, to attract females. The architecture of the bowers varies considerably from species to species. Sometimes "gardens" and "avenues" are prepared in the surrounding territory. Some of the decorations include flowers which amazingly are replaced before they wilt. Bowers have been found containing berries, shells, toothbrushes, corks, and clothespins taken from the surrounding area. Occasionally, some of these items are stolen from the bower of another bird. Some bowerbirds use fragments of

chewed bark as brushes to "paint" their arenas with the juice of fruit.

The male satin bowerbird, which looks like a crow with metallic-blue feathers, prepares an avenue with upright twigs that are 2 feet (60 cm) high. It then decorates the path with different objects, all in a shade of blue that closely corresponds to the color of its feathers. The female has rather drab feathers. When she tours the various arenas, the males become greatly involved in the arranging and displaying of their gardens. Their calls of excitement often are ignored by the female. She may look around, then simply fly away.

If the female consents, she enters the arena to mate with the male. After mating, the female flies away from the bower territory to build a nest where she rears the young by herself.

Adult males devote most of their time to decorating and protecting their bowers. They also try to destroy the bowers of other males. The competition between males gets rather intense. If a male leaves its bower for a few hours, it may return to find the bower in shambles. Then the intruder tries to take over and start building its own bower.

The elaborate courtships of the birds of paradise and bowerbirds may have evolved because the birds have never had many enemies. Naturally, this allowed more time for courting and fighting.

The Australian Everglades

The tropical rain forest changes to mangrove swamps in a region of mudflats near the coasts. A band of mangrove forest starts where the water of the coastal marshes is the deepest and the amount of salt is higher from the ocean. The types of mangrove trees found generally vary according to the amount of tidal flooding and the tolerance of these trees to salt content of the water. *Sonneratia* mangroves have polelike roots that rise out of the water like stilts. These trees are found nearer to the sea. Farther inland are mangroves of the *Rhizophora* and *Bruguiera* genuses, with roots of a characteristic elbow shape.

These large trees provide safety for many kinds of land and water birds. Some birds could live nowhere else. Among these are the mangrove kingfisher, mangrove bittern, and certain songbirds. The branches of some trees seem full of giant fruit bats or flying foxes which fly only at night in search of flowers and fruit. These bats have wingspans of 3 feet (1 m). During the day, colonies of them hang

Opposite page: A comparison of the courtship and mating habits of birds of paradise and bowerbirds is a study in contrast. Despite the differences, they evolved from common ancestors. The birds of paradise *(top three drawings)* rely on a display of their showy feathers to attract a mate. These displays evolved into more and more complicated behaviors. In the most advanced stages of their evolution, the paradise birds began to abandon the tree branches. They then began to display themselves on the ground. Next they started building arenas similar to those of the bowerbirds. The bowerbirds *(middle four drawings)* abandoned the trees at an early stage of evolution. They began building bowers that at first were simple stages. Over many thousands of years, the species continued to evolve. Now, the bowers are elaborate and lavishly decorated *(bottom three drawings)*.

The eastern and northern coasts of Australia have a band of mangrove swamps that are inhabited by interesting creatures. Among them are the mudskippers. These fish spend much of the time out of the water. They move through the mud by using their fins to hop. When in the water, they peek above the surface with their "periscope" eyes. Almost all species of mudskippers can survive for long periods out of the water. Their chief requirements are a humid atmosphere and cool temperatures. Some kinds of mudskippers can even drown if they remain too long in the water.

upside down from the branches of mangrove trees, making a continuous clamor.

Another resident of the northern coastal band of mangrove swamps is the sea crocodile. It lives in the coastal areas where the seas meet rivers. These areas, called "estuaries," are as far as 50 miles (80 km) upstream from the mouths of rivers. The crocodiles move in search of shrimp, turtles, and animals that come to drink. This species reaches 30 feet (9 m) in length. However, there are not many left, and one that large would be very rare. It can be very dangerous to humans.

Farther inland, there is another, smaller relative. It is the Johnstone crocodile, which almost reaches 10 feet (3 m) in length. These estuaries and forests also are the home of the mudskipper fish. No longer than 8 inches (20 cm), mudskippers leave the water to rest on the mud or on trees. They are able to breath outside the water because they carry well-oxygenated water in their saclike gills. These small fish are similar to the primitive fish that left the water to become the first large land animals.

Five species of this fish exist naturally in Australia. Each one occupies a different place in the marshes. The ones that live closest to the sea build mud walls to mark

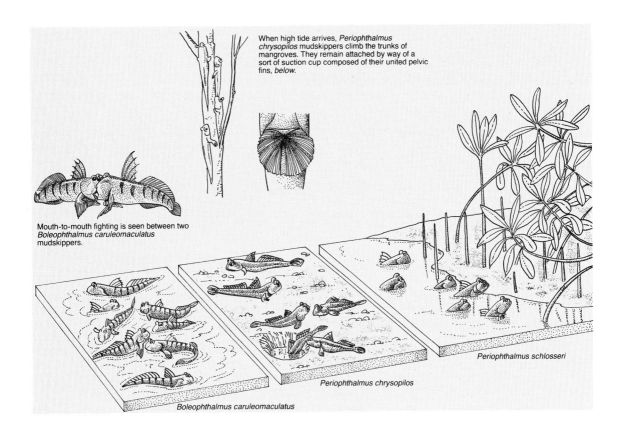

When high tide arrives, *Periophthalmus chrysopilos* mudskippers climb the trunks of mangroves. They remain attached by way of a sort of suction cup composed of their united pelvic fins, *below*.

Mouth-to-mouth fighting is seen between two *Boleophthalmus caruleomaculatus* mudskippers.

Periophthalmus schlosseri

Periophthalmus chrysopilos

Boleophthalmus caruleomaculatus

In the mangrove swamps, a number of species of mudskipper fish live in different places and follow individual diets. This way, they do not compete for food and living space. *Boleophthalmus caruleomaculatus* lives in the muddy zone nearest the sea and feeds on tiny plants present in the mud. During mating, the males defend their territories by ritualized fighting. They fight by pushing against each other with their heads. *Periophthalmus chrysopilos* lives farther inland from the coast. It escapes the waters of high tide by climbing up the trunks of mangrove trees. It feeds on insects and plants. The males dig circular holes in the mud. They attract the females to these spots by a series of small hops. *Periophthalmus schlosseri* lives in areas that are even further removed from the sea. It is a meat-eater.

their territories. The mudskippers species living farthest from the sea spend much of their time outside of the water.

In the muddy waters near the estuaries live dugongs or sea cows. The mermaids of Greek myths had the dugong's shape. Surprisingly, little is known of their habits since they are very shy and live in cloudy waters that have low visibility. However, dugongs occasionally show up during high tides when they come near the shore. They feed on underwater colonies of algae.

The dugong has a blunt, rounded snout with a bristly upper lip. The body of a dungong has a whale-like shape with a notched tail. Its flippers are used for swimming and for pushing sea grass near its mouth. The dugong is brown or gray in color. The male has two long tusks in the upper jaw, and the ends of the upper jaw bend downward.

The female dungong gives birth to one baby at a time. The dungong can grow up to 10 feet (3 meters) in length and can weigh up 650 pounds (295 km). The number of dugongs has drastically declined this century. The species is protected by law, but it is still hunted for its oil, meat, and hide.

THE EUCALYPTUS FORESTS

A group of trees called "eucalypts" is common in Australia. There are at least five hundred species. Similar plants existed in the Australian rain forest thirty million years ago. Now there are so many different kinds because ancestors of the modern trees developed within Australia. They later spread and changed to adapt to the continent's many climates. Because they are able to absorb large amounts of water, it is assumed that they originated in the tropical forest. They later changed and were able to grow in dry areas. The long, slender leaves are very oily. The oils have a strong smell that is strongest after a rain.

The Humid Areas

The eucalyptus forests of the eastern coast are crossed by short rivers that flow toward the ocean. One of these, the Hawkesbury River, has long interested geologists. The Hawkesbury River falls to the Pacific Ocean from the Great Dividing Range. Along its course are many signs of how this section of the mountain chain was formed.

The nearby plains are occasionally flooded. Then they are covered by large marshes. However, Australia's marshes and ponds tend to appear with the rains and then disappear in the dry periods. While the marshes exist, they are generally overcrowded refuges with many different kinds of animals, particularly water birds.

One of the most interesting birds is the jacana. This is a long-legged bird that can be seen walking on top of the giant water lilies. There also are black-necked storks, common white-faced herons, white herons, white ibises, and spoonbills.

The black swan is the most typical and widespread of the native Australian water birds. It stands out with its elegant shape, long neck, and black feathers. It hatches its young throughout the year. The plump, gray young toddle after their parents. During dry spells, black swans migrate to the larger ponds and lakes. Tens of thousands of them may gather.

Another bird of the changing marshes is the spoonbill duck. This bird is not the same as the shoveler, or spoonbill, of North America. It mates as soon as the rains begin to make pools. Spoonbills lay their eggs in abandoned nests. The beak is wide and long, with many small teeth at the edge. These are used to filter tiny plants and animals on the surface of the water.

A rarer species is the magpie goose, which is about the

Opposite page: The graceful jacana easily walks on water plants. Its long, thin feet distribute its weight. Jacanas are common in the eucalyptus woods of the humid parts of northern Australia. These forests are entirely different from eucalyptus forests growing in other parts of the continent. There are hundreds of species of eucalypts. Thus, there are eucalyptus forests in the humid and temperate regions with a Mediterranean climate, and in the desert and semidesert areas.

black swan

magpie goose

spoon-billed or pink-eared duck

platypus

size of a domestic goose. It has a bulge on its forehead. Its feet are only partly webbed. These birds once were killed by local rice farmers who mistakenly thought they damaged rice crops.

Along the rivers, the branches of the tall eucalyptus trees provide an ideal fishing perch for the blue kingfisher. At dawn and at dusk, the air is filled with the strange laughing call of kookaburras. These birds are bigger than the blue kingfishers, although the two are related. Kookaburras also are called "hunting kingfisher." They feed on insects, lizards, young birds, and snakes.

Near dusk, there is a great racket. The spoonbills and ibises, are fighting again.

If there is still enough light, it is possible to follow the trail of bubbles left by a swimming platypus. Eventually it will surface and mount a platform and disappear into its den. The opening of the den is generally about 7 or 8 inches (20 cm) above the water level. The platypus lives along rivers and lakes of eastern Australia from Cape York to Tasmania. It feeds on shrimp and worms. It finds its food by sifting the bottoms of lakes or streams with its sensitive bill. This soft bill is shaped like a duck's bill. The platypus is one of only two kinds of mammals in the world that hatches their young from eggs.

Birds of the Eucalyptus Forests

These forests have many birds that carry and spread the pollen of eucalyptus trees and other plants that grow there. The most abundant birds of this type are called "honeyeaters." They have long tongues with fringed edges. They feed mostly on honey and nectar. They are generally small, thin birds no bigger than pigeons.

The types of forest honeyeaters live in different ways. Some hunt insects, others suck nectar, and some eat berries. Many of them migrate, timing their travels with the blooming of the various plants from which they feed along the way. The forest plants are well suited to pollination by birds. The flower of a eucalyptus has nectar at the bottom of the flower cup. The honeyeater's beak passes through the pollen-bearing parts of the flower to reach this nectar. In the process, the pollen falls on the beak and the head of the bird. The pollen will eventually fall off the bird to fertilize other flowers elsewhere.

In June and July, the weather turns colder. Then, the male lyrebird comes out in the underbrush to display itself

white-necked honeyeater

kookaburra

lyrebird

echidna

on fallen tree trunks or on 3-foot (1 m) mounds of earth within its territory. The object is to attract females. The females seem to prefer the males that have the longest tail feathers. The males call to the females in a song that is usually high pitched and clear. But at the same time some odd notes creep in. Lyrebirds tend to imitate everything they hear, from the singing of the red-backed shrike and the laughing sounds of the kookaburra to the sounds of electric saws and factory whistles.

While the males show off by raising and spreading their long tails, the female lyrebirds are busy. They build nests, hatch eggs, and care for the chicks.

The forest underbrush also contains one of the world's most peculiar animals—the echidna. It also is called a "spiny anteater." This animal looks part porcupine, part reptile. It also has some internal similarities to birds. It has a rather low body temperature and the urinary, intestinal, and reproductive tracts all empty into a cavity called a "cloaca." Like the platypus, it also lays eggs. Egg-laying mammals are called "monotremes."

The female echidna's egg is held in a fold of skin close to the mother's belly. It hatches after about ten days. The tiny echidna remains inside this "pocket" for another eight to ten weeks. It drinks the milk that oozes from the mother's skin. When the young echidna has developed its spines to the point where the mother can no longer carry it, the baby is left in a safe place. The mother still comes to nurse it for about a year.

The echidna has other special features. One is a long and narrow mouth with a sticky tongue. This is ideal for capturing insects, a favorite food. The animal's backside is protected by many spines. In case of danger, the echidna quickly buries the bottom half of its body, exposing only its spiny backside.

Parrots

Birds also have been greatly affected by the fact that Australia is an island. The first birds to arrive in Australia evolved into interesting forms. Among these are the incredible birds of paradise, lyrebirds, emus, and cassowaries. These birds are present only in Australia and nearby islands.

As more and more kinds of birds began living in Australia, some species evolved that are very much like certain European birds. Among these are treecreepers and flycatchers. Some birds are still being introduced into Austra-

Two lemon-crested white cockatoos are pictured. These birds are named for the sound of their call. Cockatoos are among the most popular caged birds. They are kept by bird fanciers around the world. In the wild, they live in large flocks. They prefer wooded areas and forests near rivers or marshes, where they go to drink during the day. At sunset, the flock returns to its usual roosting place among the trees. They make loud sounds while fighting over the best roosting places.

Shown is a group of pink cockatoos, commonly called "galahs." The pink cockatoo is the most adaptable of the eleven species of cockatoos, which are found from the Philippines to Australia. Large flocks of these birds are found throughout Australia—even in city parks.

lia by humans. Among the most recent arrivals are the crows, hawks, and birds called "cattle egrets" that eat the insects and other parasites off the backs of oxen.

One of the most typical groups of Australian birds consists of the parrots. There are fifty-five different kinds in Australia. They live in many different places. Some eat seeds, pollen, and nectar. Others eat meat, plants, or both. All of these parrots have sturdy beaks which can be used for climbing trees. They also have four-toed feet. The first and fourth toes are turned backward. This makes it easier for the birds to grasp branches and twigs.

One group of Australian parrots is the cockatoos. They reach a length of 30 inches (80 cm). They have a crest of feathers on their heads. The color of the crest generally contrasts with the color of the rest of the body. It probably serves as an identification signal for other birds of the same species. The crest is opened and displayed during courtship rituals.

The white cockatoo and pink cockatoo (locally called "galah") are the most common. They even live in city parks. They form large groups that cluster around drinking fountains. They also feed on farmers' crops. This is partly made up for by the fact that they also eat seeds of unwanted weeds.

The yellow-tailed black cockatoo is especially important in forests. It feeds on insects that live in wood and are harmful to trees. The black cockatoos include a number of other beautiful birds that are quite rare.

There is another group of parrots called "lorikeets." They are multicolored parrots that flock to trees to feed on nectar or fruit. Rainbow lorikeets are the most common. This parrot has a green back, orange breast and crop, turquoise head, and a blue belly.

Of course, parrots are often kept as pets. They can imitate the human voice. Their colors are beautiful, and they are fairly easy to tame and keep. The desert species are particularly easy to breed in captivity. They begin to mate as soon as the humidity in the air increases.

One of the most popular desert birds is the wavy parrot. It is very noisy and sociable. The wild wavy parrot has a greenish back and nests in holes in trees. These birds are the size of a sparrow and have very long tails. They live in stands of trees in the desert. Flocks of thousands crowd around desert pools.

One of the most interesting characteristics of these parrots is their ability to postpone mating until conditions are right. They begin mating immediately after a heavy rainfall. If necessary, they will even travel long distances to find wetter areas. Thus, wild wavies reproduce at a surprising rate.

Calopsitte birds are just as common as wavy parrots. They have crests like cockatoos and slender bodies and long tails like parakeets. They frequent pools in the dry regions.

The rossella parakeets are also common. There are eight species and many subspecies. They are generally found throughout the continent. They have beautiful colors.

A crimson rosella displays its incredible colors. The rosella nests in tree cavities, usually using its beak to enlarge an existing hole. It lays its eggs in the wood chips that fall to the bottom of the cavity after the hole is enlarged. The young are dark green—perfect camouflage against the leaves. They later acquire the showy colors characteristic of the adults.

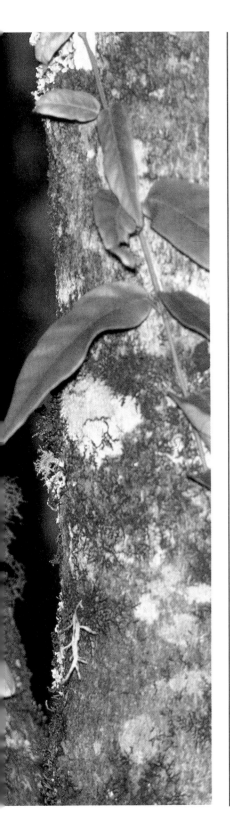

They live mostly in open forests and brush thickets, but they can adapt well almost anywhere. Just as beautiful are grass parakeets. Many of them have showy colors ranging from emerald green to bright blue.

Other Birds of the Open Forests and Thickets

Pigeons and doves are quite common in Australia. There are twenty-two Australian species and three that have been brought in. The smallest bird of this type in the world lives in Australia. It is the diamond dove, which is the size of a sparrow. It is a beautiful blue-gray spotted with white, with red rings around the eyes. Diamond doves often are kept in zoos and aviaries. They reproduce well in captivity and are nearly as popular as parrots.

Among the many birds of the open forests and dry-land thickets are the grain-eating finches. Many tame varieties of these birds have been developed around the world. Particularly well known is the mandarin diamond. This bird is no longer than 4 inches (10 cm). It has gray feathers with a striped breast and orange cheeks and beak. Almost the same size is the beautifully colored Gould diamond. Its head is red, yellow, or black. It has a bright green back, violet breast, yellow belly, and bluish undertail.

THE DESERT

Australian deserts were formed about 250 million years ago. The landscape was changed mostly by the action of wind and water. At that time, drainage was poor and water evaporated quickly. In some places, vast zones of salt flat areas were formed. From a distance, these flats glisten like broad lakes.

A number of animals live in this hostile place. One is the agamid lizard of Lake Eyre. It is a small white lizard with tiny, sunken eyes. During the hottest hours, it takes shelter under the salty crust or in the shade of ant hills. Ants are one of its main foods.

Plants that are active throughout the year in the desert have adapted to survive under very harsh conditions. Their leaves tend to be hard and leathery and are protected by wax, resin, hairs, and sometimes a coating of salt. They also are able to produce nutrients with half the amount of water required by many plants.

Most people think of a desert as a huge expanse of bare sand dunes that shift with the wind. Only about a third of Australia's deserts look like that. In the dry season, almost the only plants that can live there are the tough spinifex grasses. When the rains come, however, the desert suddenly changes. It becomes covered with flowers. But the time of blooming is short. In a few weeks, the plants wither and die. The desert once more becomes bare reddish earth. The flowers have left their seeds behind, though. When the rains return, plants and new flowers will grow again.

Animals of the Arid Zones

Desert animals have developed ways of saving water, defending themselves, and escaping enemies. Their skins, mouths, tails, claws, and even their movements seem designed for these purposes.

Several species are specialists at defense. One of these is a reptile called Gould's sand monitor. It is a lizard nearly 7 feet (2 m) long. It has long claws and strong teeth. But a thick tail is its best weapon. The monitor uses it like a club to fend off enemies. When attacked, the monitor hisses loudly while it thrashes its tail.

Some reptiles try to scare away their enemies. Two that use such scare tactics are dragon lizards and frilled lizards. The dragon lizard lives up to its name when it swells its prickly collar. The frilled lizard gets the same effect by expanding the folds of skin around its head. When these are spread out around their heads, the lizards look larger than

Opposite page: Shown is a lonely road in the Gibson Desert. The wind has not yet erased the last traces of the passing of vastly different forms of life—tire tracks and the tracks of a dog, perhaps a dingo. The Gibson Desert is located in the heart of western Australia. Its northern border adjoins the Great Sandy Desert. Areas of sand alternate with rock, prairies of spinifex grasses, and acacia woods.

bearded dragon

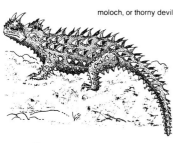

moloch, or thorny devil

leaf-tailed gecko

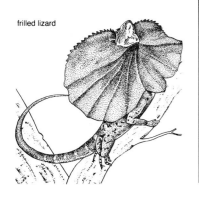

frilled lizard

they really are. They get even scarier by opening their jaws wide and making a high-pitched whistling noise. The noise alone is enough to scare off some of the reptiles' worst enemies. A different defense strategy has been adopted by the thorny devil, or the moloch. This small ant-eating lizard is completely covered with sharp spines. They look like thorns. Few meat-eaters would want a mouthful of moloch.

Far above the desert circles a number of birds of prey. These birds have sharp beaks and claws. They are excellent flyers. Because they can fly long distances, many of them are found in other parts of the world.

One of Australia's most spectacular birds of prey is the wedge-tailed eagle. A male and female protect a large territory during the reproductive period. Mating occurs after the male exhibits a series of high-diving motions in flight. It uses its powerful claws to capture herons, ducks, and rabbits. However, it feeds mostly on the bodies of dead animals. It is a scavenger of the Australian grasslands and deserts. The male and female work together to build the nest. The nest is about 6½ feet wide (2 m) and is built in a tree.

When a wedge-tailed eagle abandons its nest, the nest is sometimes claimed by a small, Australian hawk. The female of this species lays two to four eggs. This hawk is an excellent glider. It dives to capture the small mammals and lizards that it spies from above.

The Australian kestrel, a falcon, is another bird of prey of deserts and farmlands. In Northern Queensland, there are many kestrels. There, farmers set fires to clear the ground before plowing. Warm air rises from the fires. Kestrels glide in these strong air currents. They spot and capture the small mammals that run to get away from the burned areas.

Most desert birds that are not birds of prey feed on seeds and insects. They depend on pools of water for drinking. Some birds, such as the galah, a parrot, feed on seeds of plants that can live in extremely dry conditions. Therefore, these birds can stay in one area for a longer time. Others, such as the emu, must move around quite often.

Emus are the second biggest birds in the world. They are found throughout the continent. They cannot fly, but they can run very fast. They move around in search of food and water. They can eat an incredible variety of plants and insects. Emus are not appreciated by farmers since they raid farm fields. They taste anything within reach of their beaks, including bottle caps and other inedible objects.

As the sun sets, the desert becomes more tolerable.

Then it swarms with life. Many desert-dwellers are active at night. During the day, they find shelter in the ground or in the shade of spinifex bushes. There is very little fresh water, but several small marsupials are able to drink salt water from the scattered desert pools.

Desert animals store food in their dens. Others store food in the form of fat in their tails to last them through periods when food is scarce. Other animals slow down during the hottest season. This is called "estivation." The desert frogs use this method to live through the hot periods. The flat-headed chirolette, a type of frog, stores water in its bladder before burying itself in the mud to wait for more favorable conditions.

The Dingo

The dingo has adapted well to the desert. This is a wild dog with a stout head and small triangular ears that always stand up straight. The hunting habits of this meat-eater change according to how much food is available. Dingos often hunt alone. They can also form groups when food is particularly abundant or when they are after larger animals.

In the dry periods, the mother gathers all of her pups in one den. She feeds the young with grasshoppers and other insects.

Normally, the dingo lives with a family group. The mated pair cooperates in caring for the pups. The females hunt alone until the young are born. Then they spend almost all of their time with the pups, while the males get the food, defend the territory, and stand guard. There is a system of rank among the members of a group or within a family. Each member eats and drinks in a certain order.

Dingos communicate among themselves with calls that can be heard from miles away. These calls contain different messages. Certain barks attract other dingos. Others are used to signal the positions of hunting companions. Special barks call the pups or warn them of possible danger. Solitary or group howls are used to show the boundaries of territories.

Beginning eight thousand years ago when humans brought the dingo to Australia, this animal has fed on kangaroo rats and other small marsupials. Now it often hunts rabbits and occasionally even the livestock that modern Europeans brought with them.

This fact has caused war between dingos and ranchers. To protect livestock, farmers have built a long fence that begins at the southern coast of Australia and extends for 6,200 miles (10,000 km). It runs all the way to Queensland. Each 50-mile (80 km) section is patrolled by a guard armed with a rifle, traps, and poison.

A trip across the Australian desert is actually a trip through space and time. There are reminders of the history of the earth. There are plants and animals that are no different from those that lived millions of years ago. The aborigines living there remind one of distant ancestors.

THE HUMAN PRESENCE

Aborigines, the native Australians, know better than anyone on earth what it is like to live in the desert. Aborigines who choose not to live in modern society are wanderers. They move from one body of water to another. They hunt wild animals and gather wild plants. When small animals such as wallabies and lizards (and sometimes larger game like emus and kangaroos) are captured, the hunter divides most of the food with the rest of the group.

The women and children gather insects, berries, fruit, seeds, roots, and tubers. All are part of their diet. In the desert, there are harvest seasons. There is a time in which seeds and roots are plentiful, a time for the ripened kampurarpa fruit (only the sweet outer part of this fruit is eaten), and the time for the quandong (which looks like a small green tomato). Many desert plants and parts of plants are poisonous. Aborigines have ways of cooking each of them so that they become harmless.

The Culture of the Aborigines

Native Australians, or aborigines, are able to live the ways their ancestors did forty thousand or more years ago. The ways have been developed over centuries by trial and error. These people do not follow their traditions just to honor their ancestors. They do it because those methods work in the continent's harsh desert.

Over the years, explorers and settlers have praised the aborigines' ability to use things the desert provides in order to survive. In 1836, an Englishman named Charles Darwin traveled into the interior of Australia. There he met some aborigines. He said that they were very intelligent. He wrote, "In their own arts they are admirable. A cap being fixed at thirty yards distance, they transfixed it with a spear, delivered by a throwing-stick with the rapidity of an arrow from the bow of a practiced archer. . ." Darwin added that the aborigines would not cultivate the ground or build houses and remain stationary, or even take the trouble of tending a flock of sheep when it was given to them.

A century later, in 1936, a white settler crossed the Simpson Desert. Later he said there were two reasons that he was able to survive. One was that he traveled right after the rainy season, when the desert pools were full. The other was that an aborigine was with him.

The aborigines do not move about aimlessly in search of food. They do not contest the rights of others who have come into an area ahead of them. They treat guests well and

Opposite page: One of the many rock paintings of the aborigines, found in Arnhem Land. The rock art of the aborigines began 25,000 years ago with one color drawings of animals. Later, the aborigines began using more colors which they mixed from clay and plants. The powerful and friendly spirits of their ancestors are portrayed as animals. Aborigines still believe that these spirits created plants and animals.

Aborigines perform their javelin dance ritual. Almost all such dances are associated with everyday events. Subjects include the animals and birds of the desert, hunting episodes, the search for honey, and the gathering of water lilies. Only a few dances deal with such legends as the discovery of fire and death. This is said to have taken place during the "dream time" of the Rainbow Serpent.

follow strict rules about sharing.

Aborigines have very few possessions. They have a few hand-made tools. These tools are carried wherever aborigines go. They use their own hair and beards to make cords and ropes. Some clans have rules requiring members to donate their hair. The older men normally give the hair of their beards and moustaches. Their hairless faces are considered as a sign of generosity. Men without beards or moustaches are highly respected within the group. When someone is too sick or old to hunt or gather food, the others share their food with them. All the clans share their food with the eldest first.

The tools of the aborigines are decorated with drawings of the animals that they commonly see. There often are drawings of snakes, kangaroos, birds, and lizards. These drawings also show scenes of activities such as hunting and dancing. Many aborigines believe that dances and songs are given to them in their dreams by the spirits of their ancestors. There is no writing. Therefore, songs and dances are an important link with ancestors. Aborigines believe that their ancestors had supernatural energy and power. These ancestors are thought to have been giants that were part human and part animal. These beings, aborigines believe, were transformed into parts of the landscape. Some became animals, mountains, caverns, or springs, the stories say. But their energy is believed to continue. Present-day aborigines say they can tap into that energy through those objects that once were ancestors.

For example, each of the clans of a group called the Arandas, a tribe of central Australia, has picked one of these ancestral beings. As a result, there are kangaroo people, emu people, and so forth. The tie with these beings or "totems" is so strong that the women believe that their pregnancies are one of these spirits come back to life. Their children will not belong to the parents' group. Instead, they will belong to the totem that lives where the mother was pregnant.

The first exchanges that aborigines had with white people occurred when some white prisoners escaped from the prisons or penal colonies. The whites had beliefs that were very different from those of the aborigines. But the aborigines adapted to the white intruders. They worked in exchange for European "goods" such as alcohol. Aborigines tried to hang onto their way of life.

Even so, aborigines disappeared from the nearby island of Tasmania by 1876. This was only seventy years after the first white settlement. In Australia, contact with white people resulted in the spread of diseases such as flu and tuberculosis. The aborigines had no resistance to these diseases.

The population of Australian aborigines probably was 300,000 when Captain Cook claimed the continent for the British government in 1770. By the early 1900s, there were only about 30,000. In recent years, however, there has been a definite population increase. This is the result of better medical care and the creation of reservations. Some people predict a population of 300,000 aborigines by the end of this century.

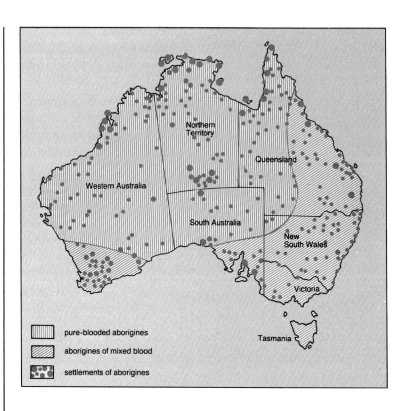

pure-blooded aborigines

aborigines of mixed blood

settlements of aborigines

The map shows where most aborigines live—pure and mixed blood. Also shown are the principal settlements. Almost all aborigines by now live in frequent contact with white communities. However, many groups have settled in desert reservations. There they keep their ancient culture and traditions. There are three hundred aborigine reservations in Australia, occupying a total area of about 110,400 sq. miles (286,000 sq. km). At first, the aborigine reservations were managed by "white" administrations. This management has now passed to the aborigines after a new government policy was started to encourage the independence of aborigines.

Changes Brought by Humans

Present day aborigines live in ways that do not abuse the environment. But this does not mean that the first humans who arrived forty thousand years ago did not affect the island's plant and animal communities. Hunting probably brought major changes. Hunting and the many fires set by the aborigines, changed the continent's plant and animal life. An example is the arrival of the dingo, a dog that probably was brought to Australia by humans about eight thousand years ago. The dingo could have helped cause the disappearance of several kinds of animals.

The biggest changes of all were caused by settlements of Europeans. The first was a penal colony at the town of Sydney. It was started in 1788. It was a place where criminals were sent to live. Later, people came to Australia to escape persecution for their religion or politics. These people built settlements on the coast or tried to move farther inland. Large areas of forest were cut to provide grazing land for sheep and other animals that were brought in.

One of the biggest disasters was the introduction, in 1859, of the wild rabbit. The rabbit found almost no enemies. The rabbits spread at a rate of 68 miles (110 km) each

Australia was discovered in 1600. In 1700, Captain James Cook officially took possession of this fertile territory in the name of the English government. From then on, immigration continued at a constant rate. The European colonization has deeply affected the population of aborigines, who were oppressed for a long period. Europeans also changed the natural balance of plants and animals. Such introductions as the European rabbit, rat, and fox changed the numbers and kinds of native species. This area in New South Wales clearly shows how the landscape has been "Europeanized" by the settlements.

year. The rabbits even began to eat all of the grass in pastures. To keep the wild rabbits under control, people introduced a disease virus (*myxomatosis*) that was deadly to the rabbits.

By 1910, approximately sixty species of marsupials had disappeared in New South Wales alone. Reasons included the destruction of their living spaces and the introduction of domestic livestock. Another animal that Europeans brought was the fox. Soon, there were foxes almost everywhere. One of the marsupials to be virtually wiped out was the rabbit bandicoot. The gray kangaroo disappeared in some areas. At the same time, some native animals actually increased in numbers. These animals prefer to live in open grasslands. These include the red kangaroo, galah, white cockatoo, magpie and lapwing. The kookaburra bird became widespread throughout Australia. It kills snakes.

Life in the bush country is hard for humans. Students are taught by radio rather than in classrooms. Mail is delivered by airplane. Often the nearest neighbor lives hundreds of miles away.

GUIDE TO AREAS OF NATURAL INTEREST

Approximately one million foreign tourists vacation in Australia each year. These visitors are mainly interested in the wildlife sanctuaries, the beautiful beaches, the Great Barrier Reef, the Australian Alps, and various areas of historical interest.

Australia's population is concentrated in a few cities that are located very far apart. As a result, there is excellent airline service within the country. However, the railway and highway systems are not as good. One of the best ways to travel within Australia is to fly and then rent a car or camper.

Those who like safe adventure may want to check with the various automobile associations that organize tours. Each participant drives according to a schedule set by a guide. (National Roads and Motorists' Association, 151 Clarence Street, Sydney, NSW 2000). Another solution is to use a private or state tourist agency which provides a wide selection of organized tours by horseback, camel, canoe or bus.

Australia has a network of adequate hotels, and motels. There are at least one hundred youth hostels. Interested persons should inquire with the Australian Youth Hostels Association, 26 King St., Sydney, NSW, 2000.

Drivers can get an international driver's license though it is not required. Drivers must remember to keep to the left and yield to the right at intersections. The largest cities are connected by four-lane paved highways. Road conditions do not permit high speeds.

There is generally little traffic away from cities. The greatest dangers to drivers are fatigue, animals that suddenly cross the road (especially kangaroos), and road conditions. In Australia, only one-fourth of all the roads are paved. There often are potholes that become puddles with each rainfall.

Before starting a tour, it is important to find out the conditions at the destination. Dryness, fires, and flooding can completely change an area within a few days. It is also advisable to carry enough food and supplies to be self-sufficient. Before entering wild country, a person should leave information and travel plans at the last police station along the way.

There are many parks in Australia. They have been established to preserve wildlife and landscapes. Not all of these areas are open to tourists. Some are centers for conservation and research.

Opposite page: Pictured is the spectacular canyon formed by the King River's slow but continuous erosion. It lies within the chain of the George Gill in the Northern Territory. On the bottom of the canyon, there is a dense cover of eucalyptus trees and shrubs that are the homes of many species of animals. The upper edge of these rock walls was dished out by the wind.

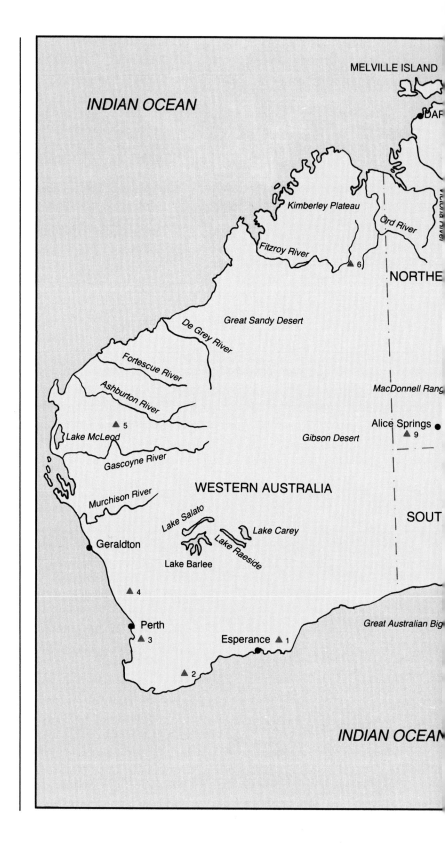

Pictured is a distribution of the main areas of natural interest on the Australian continent and the island of Tasmania.

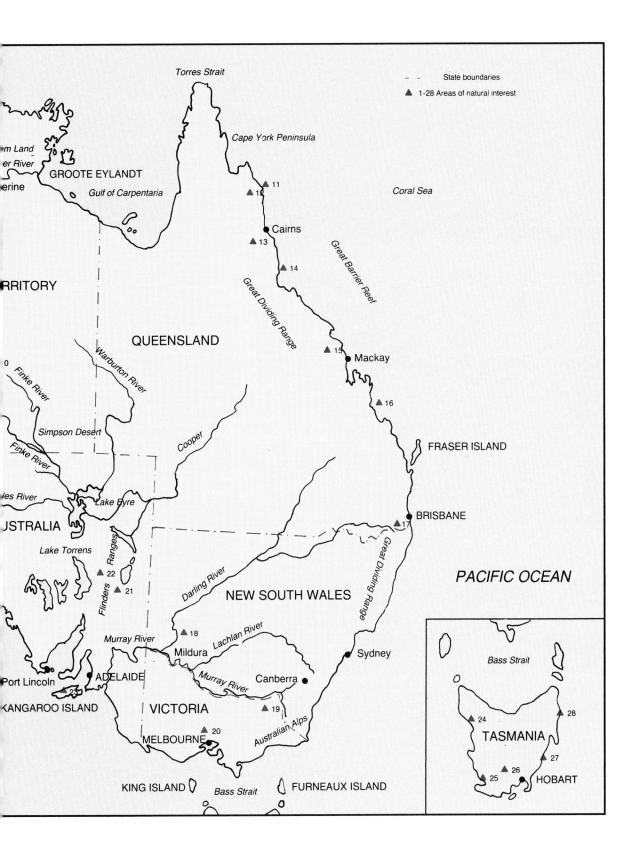

WESTERN AUSTRALIA:

Cape Arid (1)

Stirling Range (2)

John Forrest (3)

Badgingarra (4)

Barlee Range (5)

This national park of 107,854 sq. miles (279,415 sq. km) is located on the southern coast of the continent. It is 100 miles (160 km) from Esperance. There are hotels available. The beautiful flowers of this park are at their peak between October and May. There are no modern camping areas within the park.

This national park covers an area of 44,649 sq. miles (115,671 sq. km). It is located in the mountains 55 miles (88 km) from Albany. Campsites and hotels are available. One hotel and a campground park are located at Mount Barker. The park can be visited by following the scenic road that crosses the park from Chester Pan to Redgum Pass. Two recommended excursions are the ones leading to the top of Bluff Knoll (3,639 ft/1,109 m) and to Toolbrump (3,448 ft/1,051 m).

This national park occupies a general area of 609 sq. miles (1,578 sq. km) and is located 16 miles (25 km) east of Perth. It is along the Great Eastern Highway. Blossoms are the most spectacular from July to October. During the spring, the park employees organize special guided tours for visitors. They point out the plants that are typical in the area. The closest hotels and campsites are just outside Perth.

Badgingarra National Park covers 5,065 sq. miles (13,121 sq. km). It is crossed by the Brand Highway, which connects Perth to Geraldton. This highway is a few miles from the town of Brand, which offers lodging. This is one of the better-known parks in the area because of the many flowering plants which grow there.

Barlee Range National Park includes an area of about 40,300 sq. miles (104,406 sq. km). It is located approximately 150 miles (240 km) from the western coast of Australia. It is located at the same latitude as the Tropic of Capricorn. The road may not yet be completed, and the protected area may have to be visited on foot. The views of mountain gorges, flowers, shrubs, and animal life are worth the inconvenience.

The protected area is not set up for the convenience of tourists. Visitors must carry enough supplies to be self-sufficient for the duration of their stay. The park is closed during the summer.

Geikie Gorge (6)

This national park has an area of 1,210 sq. miles (3,136 sq. km). To reach it, visitors must exit the Great Northern Highway at Fitzroy Crossing and proceed for another 10 miles (16 km). This is one of the deepest gorges cut by the Fitzroy River. Although this section of the river is 186 miles (300 km) from the sea, visitors can fish for rays and other sea fish. The Johnstone crocodile, the smaller of the two species of crocodiles in Australia, lives here.

There are campsites located at the entrance of the gorge. The best time to visit this area is from May to November.

NORTHERN TERRITORY:

Kakadu (7)

Kakadu National Park covers 5,080 sq. miles (13,160 sq. km). It is located about 124 miles (200 km) east of Darwin. Many water birds live here including white herons, cranes, ducks, geese, ibises, and cormorants. Three marked trails lead to several of the numerous sites where aboriginal rock paintings can be seen. Each of these is about a fifteen-minute side trip.

Katherine Gorge (8)

This national park occupies 7,073 sq. miles (18,325 sq. km). It is located 217 miles (350 km) south of Darwin, near Katherine, which has hotels. Boat rides can be taken up the Katherine River, which flows between the steep rock walls of the gorge. From the boat, tourists can see freshwater crocodiles (Johnstone crocodiles) and patches of rain forest. The riverbanks seem to glow with the orange flowers of the eucalyptus trees. Experienced hikers can follow one of the five trails laid out on the edge of the canyon. These trails are clearly marked. Several passages are challenging and require at least a basic knowledge of rock-climbing techniques. Toward dusk, hikers might be lucky enough to see the rare and shy red-legged wallaby, the *Lophophas plumifera* dove, bowerbirds, and red parakeets feeding on the flowering eucalypts. On some of the rocks are aboriginal drawings. A camping area is located at the mouth of the Katherine Gorge.

Ayers Rock— Mount Olga (9)

This national park extends over an area of 48,708 sq. miles (126,186 sq. km). It is located 273 miles (440 km) from Alice Springs. It is reached by way of Erldunda on the Stuart Highway. This highway is a difficult road to drive. It is impassable during the rainy period. Airline service to the park is provided at Alice Springs.

Shown is a panoramic view of the Olga
Mountain area. There are thirty-one
rocky domes, all crowded close
together. They form a semicircle
covering 8 sq. miles (22 sq. km), with
Mount Olga on the west. The Olga
Mountains have low profiles because
they are very old. They have been worn
down by water and wind over millions of
years.

Ayers Rock, the large rock mass, is called "Uluru" by the aborigines. It changes color during the day as the sun moves. Until now it has been possible to climb to its highest point 1,100 feet (335 m) and explore its caverns and gorges. In the future, however, restrictions probably will be imposed. The rock is considered sacred by the aborigines. The government has returned it to them.

A tour through the surrounding mulga country will offer glimpses of many forms of desert life. There are many groups of red kangaroos and wallaroos. The wallaroo, or euro, is a kangaroo that can live for three months without drinking water, eating only spinifex grasses.

Birds likely to be encountered include wavy parrots, Bourke parakeets, and red-headed lorikeets. The chirping sounds that come from the bushes of spinifex often belong to the striped prairie wren. Like all the other desert wrens, they are reluctant to leave the safety of these spiny bushes.

The best time to visit this park is from June to October.

Finke Gorge (10)

This reserve of 17,695 sq. miles (45,842 sq. km) is located 75 miles (120 km) west of Alice Springs, by way of Hermannsburg. The road follows the Finke River for some distance before reaching the cool gorges. An incredible variety of plants grows in these gorges. Of the three hundred species of plants growing here, thirty are now considered very rare.

Ormiston Gorge is the most spectacular of the gorges. It was created by a tributary of the Finke River near one of the highest peaks, Mount Sonder. Visitors can hike between walls cut out of dark red rock. Dams of white rock with gray and black veins restrict the flow of the river, forming many natural pools. These pools attract such thirsty desert animals as the crested dove with golden wings.

One of the most scenic areas in the park is Palm Valley, which was discovered in 1872.

QUEENSLAND

Cape Tribulation (11)

Forty-three miles (70 km) north of Cairns, a reddish dirt road leads off into the lush rain forest of this national park. The road is bordered on each side by magnificent tree ferns. The park is famous for the number and variety of its plants and animals. It covers an area of 7,488 sq. miles (19,400 sq. km), extending from the coast to 3,280 feet (1,000 m) of elevation.

Cape Tribulation is one of the few areas of virgin or

unchanged forest left in Australia. Extremely rare plants grow here. Some grow only in this area. One of these rarities is a primitive plant called *Idiospermum australiense*. Its characteristics are so different from any other plant that botanists decided to classify this plant as the only member of a new plant family. There are 1,300 different species of plants that have been identified in this park.

Many birds live in the park, including lyrebirds and bowerbirds. Male bowerbirds build courtship bowers. There are several forms. Some are quite elaborate. Along the trail, many other kinds of birds appear and disappear among the trees. Underfoot, forest wrens and running birds rummage in the forest debris.

Thornton Peak (12)

This is a national park covering 900 sq. miles (2,331 sq. km). The road leads north out of Mossman. Authorized guides lead tourists on night visits in the park. The experience can provide some amazing sights and sounds. Possums move about in search of the most appetizing leaves. Flying foxes hang downward from trees. Kookaburras fly away with loud cries of alarm.

Fungi and larvae glow in the silent, humid atmosphere. The park is noted for the variety represented by its many tree marsupials. Among them are the reddish vulpine phalanger and the green possum.

Barrine and Eacham (13)

Lake Barrine National Park can be reached by following the Gillies Highway about 37 miles (60 km) from Cairns. The park extends over an area of 189 sq. miles (490 sq. km). After another 9 miles (15 km), the road arrives at Lake Eacham National Park. It covers 189 sq. mile (490 sq. km). Both of these lakes, which reach a depth of about 328 feet (100 m), are of volcanic origin. They are a paradise for bird watchers. There are about one hundred different species of birds there. Several park trails can be taken to visit the park and its rain forest. Possums often approach tourists for a handout. They are accustomed to people.

There are six different species of possums on the Atherton Plateau. The catbirds here actually mew. Catbirds and the gray-headed robin are found only in this part of Australia and in New Guinea. Neighboring Lake Barrine attracts great numbers of water birds. These include magpie geese, black swans, white herons, and ducks.

This is one of the spots in Australia where plant and animal life varies according to elevation.

Campsites and hotels are available at Cairns, Atherton, and Millaa.

Hinchinbrook Island and Nypa Palms (14)

The name of this park derives from the island on which it is located. It covers 15,189 sq. miles (39,350 sq. km). Transportation to the park can be arranged through a tourist agency in the city of Ingham. The boat trip along the canal linking Cardwell to the island goes past sandy coast and mangrove swamps. Within the island's magnificent rain forest are several waterfalls.

There is a coastal area of 2,156 sq. miles (5,585 sq. km) that has one of the most extensive and rich formations of mangrove swamps in Australia. During low tide, it is possible—but not easy—to walk among the mangrove trees.

The sights are worth the walk. There are gerigones, green-backed gerigones, and mangrove gerigones. Dark honeyeaters, mangrove honeyeaters, and collared kingfishers abound. Several kinds of nectar-eating birds appear and disappear with a whirring of wings. The most common of these birds is the yellow-breasted sunbird. It hangs its nest from tree branches.

The remains of one of the oldest palm forests is in Nypa Palms Park. It covers 1.3 sq. miles (3.4 sq. km) and lies just next to Hinchinbrook Park. It is located in the delta area of the Herbert River.

Eugella (15)

This national park spreads over 19,149 sq. miles (49,610 sq. km). It is one of the most modern parks in Australia. The name *Eungella* means "land of the clouds." The name is appropriate. The park has a high elevation, 3,280 feet (1,000 m). It is 52 miles (83 km) west of Mackay, and it is easily reached by a main road.

This area can be viewed by car from roads that cross the park. However, visitors who want to fully appreciate the beauty of the rain forest can hike on trails that lead through thick vegetation and along the river. At dusk, platypuses may—with luck—be seen along the river, along with the red-legged wallabies and gray kangaroos.

Great Barrier Reef (16)

The southern end of the Great Barrier Reef was declared a national park in 1975. In some parts of the reef, all types of activity are prohibited including camping and diving.

Several areas are equipped for overnight visitors, however. One such spot is Lady Elliot Island. Some areas are stopovers for one-day cruises from Port Douglas, and other places. In Port Douglas there are several tourist organizations that offer trips aboard well-equipped boats that cross over parts of the Great Barrier Reef.

From a glass-bottom boat, visitors can see bright colors of colonies of polyps, multicolored fish and giant clams. Four species of sea turtles or perhaps a school of young barracudas may be seen passing by.

An overnight stay on a coral islet is a great experience for any nature lover. At dawn, the shearwaters and terns leave their colonies to begin a day of fishing. At low tide, the natural pools of the coral reef teem with life. Starfish, sea cucumbers, and fish remain trapped in these pools.

Generally, summer is not a good time to visit this area because of the poisonous jellyfish. On Lowche Island, only nine miles (15 km) from Port Douglas, the Great Barrier Reef is close to the Australian coast.

Lamington (17)

Lamington National Park occupies an area of 7,681 sq. miles (19,900 sq. km). It is 60 miles (100 km) south of Brisbane. It is a rain forest where cold-climate plants and trees live alongside species typical of the warmer rain forest. For example, there are beech trees of cooler climates as well as warm-climate plants like tree ferns and orchids.

Around some of the picnic areas are forest turkeys, bowerbirds, and rosella birds. At dusk, small forest wallabies come out of the woods. Back in the dense forest, the lyrebirds give their peculiar calls. The park has campsites and hotels. The trails are extensive and well marked.

NEW SOUTH WALES

Mungo (18)

At the end of a 70-mile (114 km) stretch of rough road from Mildura, lies a rock formation called the "Chinese Walls." They mark Mungo Lake National Park. Camping is allowed. This park covers 5,422 sq. miles (14,047 sq. km).

The Chinese Walls are walls of rock that have been cut out by streams. The streams form only when it rains. This is the most important site yet discovered where there are signs of early humans. Primitive people lived on the shores of this lake until fifteen thousand years ago when the lake dried. The lack of plants has left the area exposed to the wind. Over the years, the wind has helped uncover fascinating evidence of earlier times.

Two of the most important findings were the remains of a woman who had lived twenty-five thousand years ago and

A group of wild ducks feeds in an Australian pond. The territories of northern and eastern Australia have many watering places. Some of them exist only during periods of rainfall. Others are permanent, but their water is salty. All attract many kinds of animals. The most common are birds, such as magpie geese, black swans, spoonbills, and herons.

a man's skeleton that had been painted with ochre, a red clay. The skeleton had been buried for more than thirty thousand years.

VICTORIA

Kosciusko (19)

Sherbrooke (20)

SOUTH AUSTRALIA

Flinders Range (21)

Ediacara (22)

Flinders Chase (23)

Kosciusko National Park sprawls across 243,067 sq. miles (629,708 sq. km). In winter, there is skiing on the snowy peaks. In summer, the high meadows are bright with flowers. Visitors can hike through woods of beech and other trees that are typical of colder climates. There are several mountain lakes. This area has modern facilities for tourists.

The forest of Sherbrooke is a small reserve of a few square miles. From Melbourne, it can be reached by following Highway 26 for about 25 miles (40 km) to Belgrave. Continuing towards Kalhista, the road crosses the entire protected area. This is an excellent area for watching the lyrebirds' courtship. Here the lyrebirds seem more tolerant of humans, probably because there are so many visitors. In order to see the lyrebirds, hikers must rise early in the morning during the winter season.

This national park covers an area of 30,270 sq. miles (78,426 sq. km). Here the Flinders Mountains stand out from the desert as a rough pink headland. Some areas are covered by crests of bare rock. The crests are dotted by green trees. Among the most frequently seen animals are large red kangaroos, emus, and Australian pheasants.

Brochures describe several tours and list the birds of the area. About 376 species of birds live in this park, 65 of which live on or near water. The park has a mix of marshes and lakes, desert areas with red sand dunes, and sites where aborigines once lived. Lodgings can be found near the city of Oparinna.

From Leigh Creek, where overnight lodgings are available, the road heads southeast for 26 miles (42 km) to the reserve. The reserve was an ancient seashore. It is rich with fossils of the lower Cambrian period, 550 million years ago.

Extending across 22,774 sq. miles (59,000 sq. km), this national park is located on Kangaroo Island. It is reached by ferry from Adelaide or Port Lincoln. From Kinsgate, the Playford Highway crosses the island and another road follows the southern coast. The preserve includes Cape Conedic in the center of the park.

Many animals of this island are native and live nowhere else. They have evolved in isolation. Among the most interesting animals are the wallabies, pygmy possums, and the native cat—which isn't really a cat at all. Koalas have recently been introduced onto the island. More than 120 species of birds live here, including the rare Cape Barren goose.

TASMANIA

Cradle Mountain—Lake St. Clair (24)

Cradle Mountain National Park measures 52,898 sq. miles (137,042 sq. km). It is reached out of Denport, on the northern coast, by way of Sheffield. Another route is the Lyell Highway from Hobart. The latter road completely crosses the park and then leads north. Lodgings and camp sites are available at Waldheim.

The protected area is set up for tourists. There are marked trails and skiing facilities. One of the most beautiful trails is the Overland. It crosses the park from north to south. The southern part of the trail crosses a broad plateau. The northern part passes through narrow spots between tall peaks.

Southwest (25)

Southwest National Park features 170,704 sq. miles (442,240 sq. km) of the wildest country in the region. Nearby are two areas worth visiting, even though they do not fall within the park boundary. They are the New River Laguna and Precipitous Bluff.

Derwent (26)

The sanctuary of the Derwent River includes a protected area of about 605 sq. miles (1,568 sq. km) in the section between New Norfolk Bridge and Dogshear Point. The broad estuary is inhabited by many kinds of water birds including black swans. Hobart offers lodging.

Freycinet (27)

Following pages: Shown is the desert plain that surrounds Mount Conner *(in the background)* in the Northern Territory. This mountain has an elevation of only 984 feet (300 m) above the desert floor. Its peak is formed by a rock mass that is resistant to water erosion. This mass forms a top that protects soft sandstone layers underneath from weathering.

This national park of 3,864 sq. miles (10,010 sq. km) is on a peninsula. It reaches an elevation of 2,011 feet (613 m). The granite walls form sheer cliffs facing the sea. Leading to the park, is a road to the south, off the Tasman Highway between Cranbrook and Bicheno.

Within the park are trails leading up to Mount Graham and Mount Freycinet. Below these peaks is spread a magnificent coastal landscape. There is a camping area within the park at Coles Bay.

Ben Lomond (28)

Ben Lomond is a national park of 6,190 sq. miles (16,038 sq. km). It lies in the northeastern part of the island, between Launceston and St. Mary's. It is a mountainous area and includes the two peaks: Legges Tor, which reaches 5,158 feet (1,572 m), and Stack's Bluff, with an elevation of 5,010 ft. (1,527 m). Skiing facilities are available in the winter.

GLOSSARY

aborigines the native inhabitants of a region. Australian aborigines can trace their ancestry at least as far back as forty thousand years.

adaptation change or adjustment by which a species or individual improves its condition in relationship to its environment.

algae primitive organisms which resemble plants but do not have true roots, stems, or leaves.

allelopathy a process in which plant roots release chemicals which slow the growth of other young plants of the same kind.

arid lacking enough water for things to grow; dry and barren.

aviary large cage or building for keeping many birds.

Ayers Rock the most famous hill in Australia, called "Uluru" by the aborigines.

bryozoa small aquatic animals that reproduce by budding and forming mosslike colonies.

cay a small, flat islet composed largely of coral fragments or sand.

cockatoo a type of Australian parrot. The cockatoo is characterized by a long crest of feathers on its head which is opened and displayed during courtship rituals.

concentric having a common center.

continent one of the principal land masses of the earth. Africa, Antarctica, Asia, Europe, North America, South America, and Australia are regarded as continents.

convergent evolution the adaptive evolution of physical parts, such as wings, tails, etc., in unrelated species subjected to similar environments.

coral any of several types of marine animals characterized by hardened skeletons in a wide variety of shapes.

crest a ridge or similar growth on the head of an animal.

desert a dry, barren, often sandy region that supports little or no vegetation because of the lack of rain.

dingo a wild dog native to Australia. The dingo is a desert dog, which has a stout head and small triangular ears that always stand straight up.

embryo an organism in its early stages of development, before it has reached a fully recognizable form.

emu a large Australian bird that is unable to fly.

environment the circumstances or conditions of a plant or animal's surroundings.

epiphyte a plant, such as certain orchids or ferns, that grows on another plant upon which it depends for physical support but not for nutrients.

erosion natural processes such as weathering, abrasion, corrosion, etc., by which material is removed from the earth's surface.

esophagus a muscular tube for the passage of food from the throat to the stomach.

estivation a state of dormancy during the summer or periods of drought. Desert frogs and other desert animals slow their body processes down during the hottest season in order to survive.

estuary the part of the wide lower course of a river where its current is met by the tides of the sea.

eucalyptus tall trees native to Australia with oily leaves that have a strong smell.

everglades an area of marshland, usually under water and covered in places by tall grass.

evolution a gradual process in which something changes into a different and usually more complex or better form.

extinction the process of destroying or extinguishing.

fossils a remnant or trace of an organism of a past geologic age, such as a skeleton or leaf imprint, embedded in some part of the earth's crust.

glaciers gigantic moving sheets of ice that covered great areas of the earth.

herbivore an animal that eats plants. Australia's kangaroos, phalangers, and opossums are herbivorous animals.

insectivore animals that eat insects. Australian bandicoots are insectivorous (as well as herbivorous) animals.

marsupial an animal that carries and nurses its young in a pouch on the mother's body. Some well-known marsupials are the opossum and the kangaroo.

nocturnal animals that are active at night. Owls are nocturnal animals.

omnivorous animals that eat both plants and other animals.

parasite an organism that grows, feeds, and is sheltered on or in a different organism while contributing nothing to the survival of its host.

perennial having a life span of more than two years; lasting an indefinitely long time.

photosynthesis the process by which chlorophyll-containing cells in green plants convert sunlight to chemical energy and change inorganic compounds into organic compounds.

predator an animal that lives by preying upon others. Predators kill other animals for food.

rain forest a dense evergreen forest occupying a tropical region, with an annual rainfall of at least 100 inches (54 cm).

reef a strip or ridge of rocks, sand, or coral that rises to or near the surface of a body of water.

rumen the first division of a ruminant animal's stomach, in which food is partly digested before being regurgitated for further chewing.

scuba diving a method of underwater exploration. SCUBA stands for "self-contained underwater breathing apparatus."

sediment matter or material that settles to the bottom of a liquid.

talon the claw of a bird of prey or another predatory animal. Eagles and hawks are examples of birds with talons.

tectonic plate one of several portions of the earth's crust which has resulted from geological shifting.

tern any of several seabirds related to the gull, but smaller, with a more slender body and beak and a deeply forked tail.

tuber a swollen, usually underground stem, such as the potato, bearing buds from which new plant shoots arise.

vertebrates animals having a backbone or spinal column. Fishes, amphibians, reptiles, birds, and mammals are all vertebrates, characterized by a segmented bony spinal column.

INDEX

Aborigines, 7, 9, 13, 22, 25, 26, 42, 98-102
Acacias, 20, 21
Agamid lizard, 93
Algae, 25, 33, 39, 42
Allelopathy, 71
Amphibians, 27, 29
Angelfish, 39, 40
Anti-shark nets, 43
Arandas, 101
Archerfish, 39
Areas of natural interest
    New South Wales, 115, 116
    Northern Territory, 109, 112
    Queensland, 112-115
    South Australia, 118-119
    Tasmania, 119-122
    Victoria, 118
    Western Australia, 108-109
Arid region, 23
Arkose rock layers, 26
Arnhem Land, 20, 98
Australian Alps, 9, 11, 14
Australian hawk, 94
Australian highlands, 24
Australian kestrel, 94
Australian native cat, 52
Austrosaurus, 30
Ayers Rock, 6-7, 9, 26

Bacteria, 56
Ballistes fucus fish species, 39-40
Bandicoot, 55, 103
Barracuda, 45, 46
Basaltic rocks, 25
Bearded dragon lizard, 94
Beech tree, 13
Bennett tree kangaroo, 67
Birds
    birds of prey, 94
    courtship of, 73, 76-78
    eucalyptus forests, 84-85
    groundbirds, rain forest, 72-73
    mangrove swamps, 78, 80
    open forests and thickets, 91
    parrots, 85, 88-91, 94
    rivers and marshes, 83-84
    seabirds, 40-42
Birds of paradise, 73-74, 79, 85
Birds of prey, 94
Black-necked stork, 83
Black swan, 83, 84
Black tree kangaroo, 67
Blue devil, 20
Blue eucalyptus, 13, 18, 20
Blue-green algae, 25
Blue kingfisher, 84
Blue Mountains, 18
Boleophthalmus caruleomaculatus
    mudskipper species, 81
Bowerbirds, 77-78
Broad-footed mouse, 66-67
Bruguiera genus, mangroves, 78
Brush turkey, 73, 76

Burned grass weather, 13

Calopsitte birds, 89
Cambrian period, 26
Canine phalanger, 64, 67
Capricorn Islands, 34, 35
Cassowaries, 72-73, 85
Casuarina genus, oaks, 21
Cats, 52, 54-55, 63
Cattle egrets, 88
Cays, 35-36
Central Lowlands, 9
Change
    brought by humans, 102-103
    Great Barrier Reef, 45-48
Clams, 36, 37, 46
Cleaning fish, 45, 46
Climate, 11-12
Climatic zones, 12-24
Cockatoos, 86-88, 89, 103
Cold temperate region, 14-15, 18
Cone shellfish, 36
Convergent evolution, 62
Cook, James, 101, 103
Corals, 33, 34, 35-36, 38, 39, 43-44, 45, 46
Coral Sea, 12
Courtship, birds, 73, 76-78
Craterocephalus fish species, 31
Crocodiles, 21, 80
Crown-of-thorns starfish, 46
Crows, 88
Cuscus, 72
Cycads, 13, 31
Cyclones, 12, 46

Darling River, 10-11
Darwin, Charles, 34, 35, 99
Desert frogs, 95
Desert grasses, 23
Deserts, 10, 23, 25, 31, 92-98, 99, 120-121
Devonian period, 29
Diademia sea urchin species, 40
Dingo, 53-54, 95, 97, 102
Dinosaurs, 30, 31, 32, 50
Dragon lizard, 93, 94
Dry eucalyptus forest, 20
Duckbill, 51
Ducks, 84, 116-117
Dugongs, 43, 81
Dwarf eucalyptus, 20, 22-23

Eastern Mountain Chains, 9, 11, 27
Echidna, 85
Ecology, marsupials, 53-60
Eels, 44
Elephant shark, 43
Emu people, 101
Emus, 8, 85, 94
Encounter Bay, 11
Epiphytic plants, 71
Erosion, 27
Esophagus, kangaroo, 62

Estivation, 95
Eucalyptus forests, 82-92
Eucalyptus trees, 13, 14-15, 16-17
  20, 21, 23
Evolution, 7, 18, 62, 65
  of marsupials, 49-53
Extinction, 7

Falcon, 94
Ferns, 13, 15, 18
Finke Gorge, 28
Finke River, 31
Fires
  aborigine use of, 13
  and desert vegetation, 96
  and eucalyptus trees, 23
Flat-headed chirolette, 95
Flat-headed mouse, 52
Flinders Mountains, 25, 62
Flowering plants, 23
Flycatchers, 85
Flying foxes, 78, 79
Flying possums, 69
Flying squirrel, 52
Forbidden weather, 13
Forests, 13, 15, 18, 20, 70-82, 82-92
Fossils, 7, 25, 27, 29, 34, 50
Foxes, 55, 103
Fox phalanger, 67-68
Freshwater turtles, 21
Freycinet megapode bird, 73
Frilled lizard, 93-94
Frogs, 95

Galah bird, 89, 94, 103
Gecko, 94
Genoa River, 27
Geology of Australia, 24-31
Gestation period, 65
Giant clams, 36, 37
Giant ferns, 15
Giant fruit bats, 75, 78
Giant kangaroo, 31
Gibson Desert, 92
Giles, Ernest, 31
Glaciers, 15, 35
Gogo Desert, 25
Gondwana, 29
Gould's sand monitor, 93
Gray kangaroo, 69, 103
Gray wolf, 50
Great Australian Bight, 10
Great Barrier Reef, 9, 32-48
Great Barrier Reef Marine Park, 47
Great Dividing Range, 11, 13, 14, 25,
  27, 29, 83
Green turtle, 41
Groundbirds, rain forest, 72-73
Guano, 42
Gulf of Carpentaria, 29
Gulls, 42
Gum trees, 13

Hagen wallaby, 67
Hammerhead shark, 43

Hawkesbury River, 83
Hawks, 88
Helichrysum apiculatum grass
  species, 20, 21
Herbivores, 60
Herons, 83
Hill kangaroo, 62
Honey eaters, 84, 85
Honey glider, 53
Human presence, 98-104
Humid areas, eucalyptus forests,
  83-84
Hummingbird of the marsupials, 53
Hunting kingfisher, 84
Hurricanes, 12

Ibises, 83
Insect-eating marsupials, 51, 52-53

Jacana bird, 83, 84
Jarrah trees, 18, 20
Javelin dance, aborigines, 100
Jellyfish, 33, 42, 43, 46
Johnstone crocodile, 21, 80

Kangaroo grass, 21
Kangaroo paw, 19, 20
Kangaroo people, 101
Kangaroo rats, 97
Kangaroos, 31, 52, 56-59, 60-66, 68,
  69, 72, 74-75, 103
Karri trees, 18
Kimberleys mountain chain, 26
Kingfishers, 78, 84
King River, 104
Koala, 48, 52-53, 67
Kookaburra, 84, 85, 103

Lake Eyre, 9, 93
Lapwing, 103
Laurasia, 29
Leaf-tailed gecko, 94
Liana vines, 71
Lizards, 93-94
Long-nosed bandicoot, 52
Lorikeets, 89
Lyrebird, 84-85

Macdonnell Mountains, 26-28, 30, 31
Magpie, 103
Magpie goose, 83-84
Maidenhair ferns, 18
Mako shark, 43
Mallee (impenetrable), 22
Mammal, 49-50
Mangrove bittern, 78
Mangrove kingfisher, 78
Mangrove swamps, 13-14, 78, 80-81
Mangrove trees, 78, 80, 81
Manta rays, 42, 44, 45
Marsupials, 31, 48-69, 103
Marten, 55
Matschie tree kangaroo, 66
Meat-eating marsupials, 51, 52-53,
  54, 57, 60

Mediterranean region, 18-20
Megapode birds, 73
Mesozoic period, 29, 30
Metamorphic rocks, 26, 27
Mice, 52, 63, 66-67
Miocene epoch, 31, 60
Moles, 52
Mollusks, 33, 36
Moloch, 94
Monotremes, 50-51, 53, 85
Moray eels, 44
Mound-building birds, 73
Mountain ash, 13, 15, 18
Mount Ayers, 6-7
Mount Conner, 120-121
Mount Kosciuko, 11
Mount Olga, 110
Mouse, 63
Mudskipper fish, 80-81
Mulga, 20
Murray-Darling Basin, 10-11
Murray River, 10, 11
Muttonbirds, 41
Myxomatosis, 103

Nadgee Reserve, 65
New South Wales,
  areas of natural interest, 115, 118
Nocturnal animals, 51
Noddy tern, 41, 42
Northern Territory,
  areas of natural interest, 109, 112

Oak trees, 21
Olga Mountains, 110-111
Opossums, 56, 60
Orange fish, 38
Orchids, 13, 18

Palm trees, 13, 15, 30-31
Pangaea supercontinent, 29
Parakeets, 89, 90-91
Parallel evolution, 52
Parrots, 85, 88-91, 94
Penal colonies, 101-102
Perennial plants, 23
Periophthalmus chryspilos
  mudskipper species, 81
Periophthalmus schlosseri
  mudskipper species, 81
Phalangers, 55-56, 64, 67-68
Photosynthesis, 71
Pink cockatoo, 88, 89
Pink-eared duck, 84
Placental animals, 51-52, 65
Placental marsupials, 54, 57
Plankton, 33, 45
Plant-and-animal-eating marsupials,
  51
Plant-eating marsupials, 55, 56, 62
Platypus, 49, 51, 84
Pleistocene period, 31, 35
Pneumatocysts, 42
Pollution, and jarrah trees, 18, 20
Polyps, 33, 34, 36, 42, 47

Portuguese man-of-war, 46
Pouch, marsupial, 52, 60, 65, 67
Precipitation, 11, 12
Prettyface wallaby, 67
Pygmy angelfish, 39

Queensland, areas of natural interest,
   112-115

Rabbits, 97, 102-103
Rainbow lorikeet, 89
Rain forest, 13, 70-82
Rain weather, 13
Rats, 42, 63, 97
Red kangaroo, 58-59, 61, 103
Red shark, 42
Reef shark, 42
Remoras, 42, 45
Reproductive isolation, 67
Reproductive strategies, marsupials,
   62, 63, 65-68
Rhaetosaurus, 30
Rhizophora genus, mangroves, 78
River eucalyptus, 16-17, 23
Rock paintings, 98
Rock wallaby, 62
Roseate tern, 42
Rossella parakeet, 89, 90-91
Rumen, 55

Satin bowerbird, 77, 78
Savanna, 21, 60
Scuba diving, 43-45
Seabirds, 40-42
Sea cows, 43, 81
Sea crocodile, 80
Sea cucumbers, 36, 37, 46
Sea pens, 25
Sea snakes, 44

Sea turtles, 40, 42, 43
Sea urchins, 36, 40, 46
Shark Bay, 25
Sharks, 42-43, 44
Shearwaters, 41, 42
Shellfish, 36
Silurian period, 29
Silver gull, 42
Simpson Desert, 10, 31, 99
Snorkeling, 32
Snow eucalyptus, 13, 14-15, 18
Social organization, marsupials,
   68-69
Songbirds, 78
Sonneratia mangrove species, 78
Sooty tern, 42
South Australia,
   areas of natural interest, 118-119
Spinifex grasses, 20, 22
Spiny anteater, 49, 51, 85
Sponges, 46
Spoonbill, 83, 84
Staghorn coral, 46
Starfish, 36, 37, 46
Stonefish, 38, 46
Storks, 83
Strangling fig, 71
Sweet-mouthed shark, 43

Tasmania, 11, 14, 84, 101
   areas of natural interest, 119, 122
Tasmanian devil, 53, 54, 55
Tasmanian highlands, 70
Tectonic plates, 25, 26, 29
Terns, 40-41, 42
Thorny devil, 94
Tiger-cat, 52, 55
Tourists, and Great Barrier Reef, 47
Trachyte rocks, 25

Tree kangaroo, 62-63, 66, 67, 72,
   74-75
Triassic period, 27
Tropical fish, 38-40
Tropical region, 13-14
Trunk fish, 38
Tuart trees, 18
Tuna, 41, 45
Turtles, 21, 40, 41, 42, 43

Uluru, 6-7, 9, 26

Victoria,
   areas of natural interest, 118
Virginia opossum, 60
Volcanoes, 25
Vulpine phalanger, 67-68

Wallabies, 62, 67
Warmed up weather, 13
Water birds, 21
Wavy parrot, 89
Wedge-tailed eagle, 94
Western Australia,
   areas of natural interest, 108-109
Western gray kangaroo, 69
Western Plateau, 9
White cockatoo, 86-87, 89, 103
White-faced heron, 83
White heron, 83
White ibis, 83
White-necked honey eater, 85
Wobbegong shark, 43
Wolf, 50, 54
Wombats, 31
Worms, 33
Wreck Island, 34

CREDITS

MAPS AND DRAWINGS. G. Vaccaro, Cologna Veneta (Verona), Italy. **PHOTOGRAPHS. C. Giacoma,** Turin: 27, 41, 44-45. **Marka Graphic,** Milan: 21, 34-35, 120-121, cover; Dallas & Heaton 48, 69; C. Mauri 22-23, 95. **G. Mazza,** Montecarlo: 53, 90-91. **L. Oltolina,** Morbio Inferiore: 88-89. **Overseas,** Milan: T. Fontes 32, 38-39, 40; C. Wolinsky, 19; Explorer/J. Ferrero 6-7, 14-15, 16-17, 20, 24, 28, 30-31, 70, 96-97, 100-101, 104, 110-111; Explorer/M. Seares 103; Jacana 64-65; Jacana/J.P. Ferrero: 54-55; Jacana/Labat 58-59, 86-87; Jacana/J.P. Varin 61, 66, 74-75, 76; Oxford Scientific Films/J. Cooke 80; Oxford Scientific Films/A.G. Wells 63. **Panda Photo,** Rome: A. Bardi 98; C. Consiglio 72; A. Petretti 47; L. Sonnino Sorisio 37; M. Sonnino Sorisio 10-11. **D. Pellegrini,** Milan: 57, 77, 82, 92, 116-117.

DATE DUE

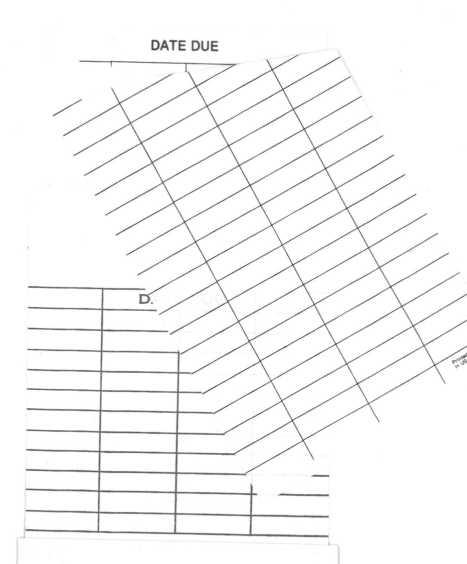